FIFTY UNCOMMON BIRDS
OF THE UPPER MIDWEST

A Bur Oak Book

FIFTY
UNCOMMON BIRDS
OF THE UPPER MIDWEST

Watercolors by Dana Gardner

Text by Nancy Overcott

UNIVERSITY OF IOWA PRESS

IOWA CITY

University of Iowa Press, Iowa City 52242

Copyright © 2007 by the University of Iowa Press

www.uiowapress.org

All rights reserved

Printed in China

Design by Omega Clay

The University of Iowa Press is a member of Green Press Initiative and is committed to preserving natural resources.

Printed on acid-free paper

Library of Congress Cataloging-in-Publication Data

Gardner, Dana.

 Fifty uncommon birds of the upper Midwest / watercolors by Dana Gardner; text by Nancy Overcott.

 p.   cm.—(A Bur oak book)

 Includes bibliographical references and index.

 ISBN-13: 978-1-58729-590-4 (cloth)

 ISBN-10: 1-58729-590-3 (cloth)

 1. Birds—Middle West. I. Overcott, Nancy. II. Title.

QL683.M55G37 2007

598.0977—dc22   2006038075

07 08 09 10 11 C 5 4 3 2 1

In memory of
ALDEN F. RISSER

CONTENTS

INTRODUCTION

A rising, three-part musical trill sends my heart racing, but until my brain catches up to my heart, I don't realize that the song is coming from a cerulean warbler. Soon a very small bird with a sky-blue head, back, and breast band appears near the top of a tree in Beaver Creek Valley State Park in southeast Minnesota. The sighting is unusual because this warbler has experienced a dramatic decline due to the loss of the large, mature hardwood forests that are its natural habitat.

For this book, which complements our *Fifty Common Birds of the Upper Midwest*, Dana Gardner and I selected species that are uncommon because of dwindling populations, species that may be common elsewhere but not in the Upper Midwest, species that may be abundant one year and absent the next, and species that frequent our region but are uncommonly seen.

Another species that fits into the low population category is the red-headed woodpecker, a bird with a striking red head, white wing patches, and blue-black back that once flew vigorously from tree to snag to utility pole in any open area with large scattered trees from the East Coast to the edge of the Great Plains. Because of habitat loss and other threats, this woodpecker has experienced a fifty-percent decline in population over recent decades and a sighting is now no ordinary event.

Eastern and western meadowlarks, closely related grassland species that we present together, also suffer from habitat loss. Their sudden bursts of bubbling spring songs reach our ears less frequently than they did only a couple of decades ago.

A relatively common bird of western marshes that wanders widely, although usually not east of the Dakotas, is the white-faced ibis. In April 2005, this strange-looking heron-like creature with glossy chestnut and greenish feathers, a white border around its red facial skin, and a long, decurved bill was foraging on an island in Cardinal Marsh, a state wildlife area in northeast Iowa that provides sanctuary to hundreds of wetland creatures. The ibis was new to me but not to my friends Carol Schumacher and Fred Lesher, who quickly identified it.

Bohemian waxwings may also wander widely, especially in winters when berries are scarce in their normal ranges of western Canada, the western states, and northern Minnesota. On December 29, 2000, when I found seven Bohemians in my crabapple tree, Dana, who was visiting nearby in his hometown of Lanesboro in southeast Minnesota, did not come to see them because he felt sure that he would find them on his upcoming trip to Duluth to witness the northern owl irruption. Unfortunately, he found no Bohemians on his trip and is still waiting for his first encounter with this species.

Speaking of northern owls, while driving home from Winona, Minnesota, in December 1996, I passed a white apparition on top of a utility pole. Curious to learn if my eyes were tricking me, I turned around, drove back to the pole, and found a snowy owl, still as a statue except for an occasional blinking of its big yellow eyes. Later, when more snowies appeared in our area, we recognized that it was an irruptive winter for these owls, who move south from Canada and the Arctic tundra searching for food in years when their usual fare of lemmings is in short supply.

Notorious for their irregular abundance are the sparrowlike dickcissels, which, being particularly sensitive to the effects of rainfall on habitat, may occur by the hundreds in a certain area one year and be absent the next. In the summer of 2004, a dickcissel in the Upper Midwest was an uncommon sighting, but in 2005 and 2006, the males with their black Vs above yellow breasts sang their names from fence posts, power lines, and weed stalks in every farmer's field.

A bird that is uncommonly seen but whose descending whinny is a signature sound of wetlands is the sora, a rail whose narrow body and cryptic plumage allow it to move invisibly through marsh grasses. Because of their nocturnal habits, black-crowned and yellow-crowned night-herons, which we portray in a single account, are also infrequently observed. The yellow-crown's inaccessible habitats make it harder to find than its relative. The brown creeper, a regular spring and fall migrant in our area, is difficult to see because of its small size, barely audible high *seee* note, plumage that looks like bark, and habit of spending most of its time crawling up trunks of trees. Another regular migrant is the small, plump winter wren, whose brown coloring and habit of foraging low to the ground among rocks and roots near small streams hide it from most eyes.

Of these and the thirty-nine other species that Dana and I chose, many are familiar to us, while others have made rare appearances in our lives. To portray each bird in a manner that offers a feeling for its personality and the way it lives its life, we include personal anecdotes and information drawn from our own observations and research. In addition, especially for the species with which we are least familiar, we rely on the stories and expertise of others, thus allowing us to acknowledge some of the best birders in the Upper Midwest. A few of these people have personally inspired us and added to our love of birds, which began for both of us in the rich habitats of the Big Woods around Lanesboro, where Dana spent his childhood and where I moved with my husband at the age of thirty-five.

Dana's interest in watching, drawing, and painting birds began at the age of seven. Through his high school years, he pursued these endeavors alone with the encouragement of his parents. After leaving Lanesboro, he studied biology at the University of Minnesota. There he met David Parmalee, a prominent ornithologist, artist, and then director of the university's field biology station at Lake Itasca, who encouraged Dana to develop his artistic talents by allowing him to design his own field illustration course at the station, which Parmalee ably supervised. Support also came from Bob Janssen, who published many of Dana's early paintings and drawings in the *Loon*, the journal of the Minnesota Ornithologists' Union, which Janssen edited for many years.

After graduating from the university and while serving as a soldier in the former Panama Canal zone, Dana met the renowned American ornithologist Alexander Skutch. When Skutch saw his depictions of tropical birds, he invited the young artist to visit him on his Costa Rican farm and to become the primary illustrator of his books. There followed endless opportunities for studying, drawing, and painting tropical nature through annual trips to Skutch's farm along with extended visits in other parts of Central America, South America, and Southeast Asia.

In the meantime, Minnesota's Fillmore County, especially the Lanesboro area, began attracting artists and nature lovers to its beautiful wooded valleys. When Dana learned of this support and outlet for artists, he happily returned to exhibit his work in the community he had left thirty-five years earlier. At about the same time, he renewed contact with Holly Carver, director of the University of Iowa Press. Because she was familiar with his work from her years at the University of Texas Press, where many of Skutch's books were published, Holly provided Dana with a venue for publishing paintings of the birds from his childhood and, after reading some of my essays, gave me the opportunity to collaborate with him.

Like Dana, I began as a solitary birder. Then in 1987, after pursuing the hobby on my own for three years, I joined the Minnesota Ornithologists' Union. When Anne Marie Plunkett, a bird enthusiast from Rochester, learned of my membership, she immediately contacted me. Because she had been studying the diaries of Johan Hvoslef, Lanesboro physician and naturalist who recorded all the wildlife he saw in Fillmore County from 1881 to 1918, she had a particular interest in my area. Our meeting led to the county's first Christmas Bird Count in 1988 and the formation of the Fillmore County Birders club in 1989. For twenty years now, Anne Marie has been not only a good resource but a good friend as well.

The most experienced member of the Fillmore County Birders was Alden Risser, a physician from Stewartville, who in 1929 helped found the Upper Mississippi Bird Club, which soon became the Minnesota Bird Club and in 1938, after joining with two other groups, the Minnesota Ornithologists' Union. Dr. Risser's greatest role, however, was as a mentor to many young birders and a few adults, including me. He taught his students about vocalizations, habitats, and behaviors and instilled in them an appreciation for all of avian life, whether common or uncommon. On December 5, 1999, our friend and teacher passed away. I know I can never see Doc again, but I still half expect to wake up on a Saturday morning, look out my kitchen window, and find him with his eager young protégés standing in my driveway, binoculars to their eyes.

One of Doc's protégés is John Hockema, who is known for his ability to identify species by the slightest sounds and briefest of appearances and on whose expertise I frequently rely. Two dear friends and frequent hosts to the Fillmore County Birders were Gordon and Mary Jo Dathe of Spring Valley. Gordy died on April 7, 2006, while watching woodpeckers, chickadees, and nuthatches at his suet feeder from his favorite chair by his front window.

Two good companions, Carol Schumacher of Winona and Fred Lesher of La Crosse, Wisconsin, have generously spared time from their busy schedules as field trip leaders and ardent conservationists to teach me much of what I know about the avian world as we have explored parts of Iowa, Wisconsin, and Minnesota together. Three Iowans, with whom both Dana and I have spent happy hours in the field, are longtime birder Dennis Carter, Luther College ornithologist Tex Sordahl, and my good friend Mary Lewis, who brought the five of us together.

All of these people have expressed concern about the fate of birds and with good reason. BirdLife International's 2006 report shows that more than a fifth of all species worldwide face possible extinction. According to the National Audubon Society, as of 2006, twenty-five percent of species in the United States are declining significantly.

One of the greatest threats to these beloved creatures is an alarming decrease in biodiversity. Agricultural monocultures and single-species tree farms are replacing or fragmenting the habitats that are necessary for many birds. Genetically modified organisms are crossing species barriers and contaminating gene pools, leading to a loss of genetic variation and possible extinction of the native plants that are also necessary for many birds. Pesticides and herbicides are adversely affecting the plants and insects that are beneficial to birds while increasing resistance among targeted species. Fortunately, a few birds, including downy woodpeckers, blue jays, chickadees, robins, chipping sparrows, red-winged blackbirds, and orioles, have adapted to some of these changing conditions.

The species that are in greatest peril are the specialists, such as grassland birds, whose ecosystems have suffered the most damage. The once vast prairies in the United States have been lost to agriculture and urban development, as have increasingly large grassland areas in Central and South America, leading to a decline in the Swainson's hawk, greater prairie-chicken, upland sandpiper, dickcissel, grasshopper sparrow, Henslow's sparrow, bobolink, eastern meadowlark, western meadowlark, and others. Shrublands have also given way to human expansion, thus creating problems for species like the brown thrasher, yellow-breasted chat, and lark sparrow that thrive in such areas.

Forest ecosystems are suffering too. Trees in the western hemisphere are actually increasing in number, but they consist mostly of limited species produced for harvest and second-growth trees such as poplars, willows, and alders that support birds such as the Philadelphia vireo, American redstart, field sparrow, and American goldfinch. However, demands for lumber, paper, and development have greatly reduced the once large tracts of old-growth deciduous forests, coniferous forests, and rainforests that many warblers, thrushes, and owls require and the swampland woods that yellow-crowned night-herons,

Acadian flycatchers, and prothonotary warblers prefer and where the great ivory-billed woodpecker once raised its young. From 2004 through 2006 possible sightings of the ivory-bill in the Big Woods of Arkansas's Mississippi River Delta and along the Choctawhatchee River in the Florida panhandle raised hopes that the ivory-bill, thought to be extinct, might still exist. Although the evidence is insufficient for confirmation, scientists are optimistic that future searches in Arkansas, Florida, and other southern states will provide definitive proof that the elusive woodpecker prevails.

Over the last two hundred years, more than half of the wetlands in the United States have been depleted by water diversion for use by cities and agriculture or filled in to create land for human infrastructure, leading to a decline in waterfowl, herons, rails, cranes, shorebirds, and a variety of passerines.

Although grasslands, shrublands, woodlands, and wetlands still exist, many are in fragmented patches that are too small to maintain healthy, diverse populations of plants and animals. Woodland fragmentation is particularly troublesome for deep forest birds because it forces them to nest closer to woodland edges, where they are more vulnerable to predation by edge-loving crows, jays, raccoons, and other animals. They are also vulnerable to brood parasitism by the brown-headed cowbird, which never makes its own nest but lays its eggs in the nests of other species, thus contributing to the decline of those it parasitizes, including members of the flycatcher, vireo, thrush, and warbler families.

In addition to all of these precarious situations are the looming threats inherent in global climate change. Among other possible impacts, scientists predict that global warming will alter habitat type and food availability. Migratory birds in particular, some of which are already migrating earlier in response to increasing temperatures, may find that the timing of their arrival on breeding grounds no longer coincides with the availability of the fruits, nuts, insects, and other foods that they need to survive or the nesting material and nesting sites that they need in order to breed successfully.

Predation by domestic cats, destruction of nests and nestlings by early mowing of hay fields, barbed wire fences, discarded plastic bags, pollution, and collisions with windows, towers, and electric wires represent a few of the other perils that birds encounter.

However, the avian world has shown a resiliency to changing conditions over the millennia and some of the species that appear to be in trouble now may surprise us. In addition, conservationists, seeing the dangers, have mounted an unprecedented effort to help birds through research, education, and habitat protection. Research has shown that the best approach is to recognize trouble early and try to stabilize populations while a species is still relatively common. Preservation programs must not only save breeding areas as they have in the past but wintering grounds and migratory stopovers as well, which frequently involves international cooperation.

An example of this sort of cooperation is the creation by the American Bird Conservancy and the Colombian conservation group Fundación ProAves of a five hundred–acre preserve of subtropical forest in Colombia to protect the cerulean warbler. Another international effort is the Western Hemisphere Shorebird Reserve Network, which has identified and encouraged the preservation of four million acres of wetlands between Argentina and Alaska on which migratory shorebirds depend. Our National Audubon Society works in partnership with BirdLife International in a number of ways, including promotion of the Important Bird Areas program, which identifies the most critical habitat sites worldwide. And the Nature Conservancy works with partners, corporations, and indigenous people to protect the most ecologically important lands and waters worldwide. In response to recent emphasis on the need to connect areas of intact habitat, thus facilitating species movements necessary for reproduction and survival, the Nature Conservancy has been instrumental in creating more than eight hundred ecological corridors.

National organizations, such as the American Ornithologists' Union, Cornell Lab of Ornithology, National Wildlife Federation, and Ducks Unlimited, which recently announced a large wetland initiative, offer help as well. National wildlife refuges and parks; state, county, and city parks; and yards landscaped for wildlife also provide essential habitat. State nongame wildlife programs fund research and manage critical habitat. Statewide birding organizations maintain seasonal reports submitted by members, publish journals, and organize field trips. Audubon's Christmas Bird Counts, which take place all across the Americas, are a way for citizen scientists to contribute information regarding distribution and frequency. Likewise for Cornell's Great Backyard Bird Count and the North American Breeding Bird Surveys, a project of the U.S. Geological Survey and the Canadian Wildlife Service.

These efforts represent only a few of the ways that people are helping birds. For more information, see the annotated reading lists following the species accounts.

In spite of all the research, education, and preservation devoted to birds, we have already lost some species and will certainly lose more. Although the state of the world's birds inspires little optimism, I still have hope for these fragile yet sturdy creatures. And I know it is not too late to experience the excitement of migration, the return of the wood thrush with its eloquent songs or the common loon with its wacky laughter. It's not too late to witness the fledging of red-headed woodpeckers, the booming of prairie-chickens, or the winter arrival of snow buntings.

Through our presentations, from the surf scoter with its multicolored bill to the gregarious evening grosbeak that looks like a giant goldfinch, Dana and I hope to give our readers the desire to look for these uncommon birds, the information necessary to find them, and the will to protect them.

FIFTY UNCOMMON BIRDS
OF THE UPPER MIDWEST

Surf Scoter

Melanitta perspicillata

On December 8, 2004, I joined my friends Carol Schumacher and Fred Lesher to look for waterfowl along the Mississippi River north of Winona, Minnesota. The river was not yet frozen and we found tundra swans just where we expected to see them. In the main channel were thousands of common mergansers. Closer to us was a common loon.

Not far from the loon were two ducks that looked different from ducks we were used to seeing. By noting their low position in the water, the way they sprang forward and dove with wings partly spread, their white face patches, stout bills, and dark appearance, Carol and Fred, who know waterfowl better than I do, were able to identify the birds as scoters, sea ducks that are rare for this area. The lack of white wing patches told us they were surf rather than white-winged scoters. Brownish rather than black bodies and the lack of multicolored bills meant they were females or first-winter juveniles.

Although unrelated to the American coot of the rail family, these birds have acquired the nickname sea coot, perhaps because, like coots, they are dark waterbirds not good for eating. Unlike coots, they spend much of the year in large concentrations on the coasts, frequently scoting, or scooting, through breaking waves while feeding offshore where they consume primarily mollusks but also small fish, crustaceans, and aquatic insects.

Scoters occasionally winter on the Great Lakes and, rarely, on other bodies of fresh water. Most of the birds seen away from the coasts are migrating. The birds we saw on the Mississippi were likely on their way to the Gulf of Mexico. I was happy their rest stop coincided with our visit, thus allowing me to add another species to my life list.

As with other ducks, surf scoters form new pair bonds each year, commonly on their wintering grounds. In courtship the male bows, swims with his neck stretched upward, and sometimes pursues a female underwater. Breeding takes place in northern Canada or Alaska. Scoters must breed in freshwater areas because their young, whose specialized salt glands are not fully developed, cannot survive drinking salty water. The female, who also does all the incubating, builds a nest lined with down in a shallow depression near a pond or sluggish stream in sparsely forested habitat and sometimes on open tundra. Shortly after hatching, the babies go to water and feed themselves, although their mother remains nearby for several weeks. Young birds eventually form in larger crèches attended by one or more adults. They will not breed until they are two or three years old.

This species declined seriously in the early 1900s, possibly due to overhunting. Persecution of sea ducks is common because of their perceived impact on fish. They are also vulnerable to oil spills and other pollution. However, current populations appear to be stable.

Hooded Merganser

Lophodytes cucullatus

From a distance, because of its large, white head patches, I sometimes mistake a male hooded merganser for the smaller male bufflehead. However, the white on the bufflehead continues around the back of his head, while the merganser has two patches, one on each side. The black vertical bars that separate his rusty flanks from his white breast further distinguish the merganser. The female has a rusty-orange crest and brownish body. The striking crests and elegant plumage of these ducks always startle me.

Two other mergansers, the common and the red-breasted, inhabit North America. All have serrations on the edges of their bills that enable them to grasp slippery fish, thus earning them the nickname sawbills. Mergansers belong to the subfamily Mergini, which also includes sea ducks such as eiders, scoters, goldeneyes, buffleheads, and long-tailed ducks. All Mergini have a tolerance of salt water and prefer animal foods that they find by swimming underwater while propelling themselves with their feet.

The hooded is the smallest of our three mergansers and seems to be the least common because it usually appears with only one or a few other birds and because it inhabits swamps, wooded ponds, narrow rivers, or coastal estuaries where it is difficult to observe. I once saw a pair on the South Fork of the Root River near my home, but most of the birds I've seen have been on backwater ponds of the Mississippi River, such as those along Army Road outside of New Albin, Iowa.

Pairs form in late fall or winter. During courtship the male dramatically raises and spreads his crest. Breeding grounds are generally across the Northeast to the Upper Midwest, into Canada, and south along the Mississippi. The female builds a nest of wood chips lined with down in a tree cavity near water ten to fifty feet above ground. Females often lay eggs in each other's nests, may share incubation with other cavity nesters, and occasionally hybridize with goldeneyes and buffleheads. Incubation lasts about one month. Within twenty-four hours after hatching, the young leave the nest, not by being pushed out or carried by the mother as formerly thought but by jumping to the ground when she calls from below. The babies feed themselves, while their mother watches over them. They are able to fly when they are about seventy days old.

Migration to the southeastern states and the northern coast of Mexico occurs late in fall. The birds usually arrive in pairs or small flocks, then gather into single-species roosting groups of one to two hundred.

Hooded mergansers declined in the past with the loss of large, mature trees near water, which they require for nesting. However, because they have adapted to the use of nest boxes, such as those provided for wood ducks, populations are presently rising.

Greater Prairie-Chicken

Tympanuchus cupido

In spring male greater prairie-chickens, also known as pinnated grouse, gather on traditional display grounds called leks. In urgent attempts to attract females they engorge the yellow combs above their eyes; raise their pinnae, or elongated earlike feathers; inflate their orange esophageal air sacs; and emit low hooting moans or booms as the sacs deflate. Minnesota birder Mark Alt described the display he witnessed in west central Minnesota as a "foot stomping, whoop yelling, balloon sac resonating, cluck stammering ritual."

Several times in the 1970s, my birding partner Fred Lesher visited Fred and Fran Hamerstrom in an area of central Wisconsin now preserved as Buena Vista Prairie, thanks to efforts by the Hamerstroms. At dawn, Fred would find himself in a blind watching prairie-chickens boom and "carry on like so many windup toys, stamping and drumming their feet as they scurry about, and occasionally leaping vertically while uttering a squawk."

After mating, the female lays and incubates ten to twelve eggs in a shallow depression among tall grasses. The young hatch in about twenty-four days and quickly leave the nest to eat seeds, leaves, and insects they find for themselves, although they stay with their mother for almost three months. The birds may remain in the same area year round or travel up to a hundred miles between their breeding and wintering grounds.

The greater prairie-chicken was once abundant across eastern and central North America. However, according to Thomas S. Roberts in his comprehensive 1932 book *The Birds of Minnesota*, this species had not yet arrived in our region during the early days of exploration. In the mid 1880s, keeping pace with settlement, clearing of forests, and planting of grain fields, it extended its range west and northwest. The bird's preferred habitat is tallgrass prairie, but it adapted to cultivated grasses and eventually entered cultivated areas interspersed with stands of oak.

On April 12, 1883, Johan Hvoslef, Lanesboro physician and naturalist, wrote, "The prairie-chickens boomed so loudly this morning from Henrik's field that we could hear them very plainly in town." He reported these birds until 1918 when his diaries ended. By the late 1930s, the species had disappeared from southeast Minnesota.

Roberts lamented the extensive hunting of prairie-chickens and warned that without some restraint they were destined to the same fate as the now extinct passenger pigeon. In Minnesota, 410,000 birds were taken in 1925 alone. Habitat loss due to an increase in the size of cultivated fields, leaving no hedgerows for cover and no residue of prairie plants, also contributed to the decline of the species, which is now primarily confined to preserved native grassland in the Midwest. Populations could rise with restoration of additional habitat, but that is unlikely to occur given the demands of agriculture.

Common Loon

Gavia immer

The many popular recordings of common loons cannot begin to compare with the rich yodeling of actual birds on a summer night in the north woods. A feeling for what wildness is must be similar in all of us, because "wild" is the word we most often use to describe this music that sends quivers of delectable fear through our bodies. To some it sounds like demented laughter, giving rise to "loony" as a colloquial term for madness.

Loons, five species in all, are the only members of the family Gaviidae and the order Gaviiformes. Their relationship to other birds is unclear. For decades the American Ornithologists' Union listed them as our oldest species, which may have influenced my impression that they look primitive. That impression continues despite the AOU's 2004 determination through genetic studies that loons have in fact evolved more recently than geese, swans, ducks, partridge, and grouse.

Common loons are bulky, low-slung, fish-eating divers with good underwater vision and legs set far back on their bodies for propulsion in the water. To locate fish, they peer into the water with bills and eyes submerged, then dive and swim below the surface. The position of their legs makes them awkward on land, where they move by pushing themselves along on their breasts. They need large lakes with ample room for takeoff because their heavy bodies require running starts to fly.

On lakes and tundra ponds in Canada, Alaska, and the northern tier of states from Minnesota to the East Coast, loons claim breeding territory by yodeling and circling overhead. In synchronous displays the male and female chase, swim, dive, and lower their bills into the water. The nest, built by both sexes, is a mound of vegetation on an island or shore. Both sexes incubate their two eggs for about two weeks. The young leave the nest soon after hatching, but their parents continue to feed them and often carry them on their backs. Flight occurs about ten weeks after hatching.

The common loon is Minnesota's state bird, although it breeds only in the central and northern regions. During migration, however, it occurs on large bodies of water throughout the state and across the country. In 1932 ornithologist Thomas S. Roberts wrote that the loon once nested on every large lake in the state. He lamented its decline due to excessive hunting in spite of its unsuitability for eating.

This species is presently threatened in several states and Canadian provinces. Reductions in population are related to human disturbance on breeding grounds, poisoning from lead fishing tackle, water pollution by industrial wastes, and oil spills on the coasts where it winters. Education efforts have resulted in some decrease in human disturbance and the use of lead fishing tackle, but the other dangers are more difficult to mitigate.

American White Pelican

Pelecanus erythrorhynchos

Their great white bodies, huge yellow bills, and black flight feathers on wings spanning nine feet make American white pelicans look as much like storybook characters as living creatures. Every fall during Hawk Watch Weekend at Effigy Mounds National Monument near Marquette, Iowa, a flock of these birds circles overhead. Although we are watching for migrating hawks riding updrafts off the bluffs of the Mississippi River, the pelicans always interrupt this endeavor. We stop to admire their choreography as they circle and turn in unison, the sun glinting off their immaculate whiteness.

White pelicans are present along the Mississippi during migration. Nonbreeding birds, which tend to travel widely, are also present there in the summer. I have often seen these birds from Trempealeau National Wildlife Refuge north of La Crosse, Wisconsin, where I have been able to observe their synchronized foraging methods. Sometimes they swim in a semicircular formation, herding fish, their primary food, toward the shoreline where they can easily catch them. Or two groups, mirroring each other, may drive prey into a narrow space between them. Flocks will also move in unison across the water, catching fish in the huge expandable pouches under their long bills.

Pelicans are colonial breeders. To nest successfully, they require freshwater lakes undisturbed by predators or humans. Mating displays include bowing, strutting with heads erect and bills pointed down, and flying in circles. Both sexes build a nest on the ground in a scrape rimmed with dirt, stones, and plant material. Both parents incubate the two eggs for about a month. Because they are among the few species that do not develop brood patches—bare sections of skin on the abdomen or breast that transfer body heat to eggs—pelicans incubate their eggs on or under their feet. Nestlings receive food from both parents; unless the food supply is abundant, the second baby to hatch doesn't survive. After about three weeks, the young leave their nests and gather with other young birds. They are able to fly about ten weeks after hatching.

In fall, white pelicans migrate in flocks to their wintering grounds in northern Mexico and along our southern coasts, where they may encounter their cousins, the brown pelicans, a species that rarely strays inland.

Previously, the white pelican bred broadly across interior North America, including the states of Wisconsin, Minnesota, and South Dakota, in which they rarely nest now. Today, breeding regularly occurs in Alberta, Manitoba, Saskatchewan, Montana, and North Dakota. Although by the mid twentieth century this bird had become an endangered species, increased protection of its habitat has enabled populations to rise. In most areas, however, it remains a species of special concern.

American Bittern

Botaurus lentiginosus

The bird stood still, like a stick, with its neck stretched up and bill pointed toward the sky. Its frozen position and vertical stripes blending with the lights and shadows of marsh grasses made it almost impossible to see even when I was looking directly at it. I was participating in the May 1989 Minnesota Ornithologists' Union weekend along the Mississippi River in Winona and Houston counties. I had never seen an American bittern before, and this one would have escaped me without the help of our leader Kim Eckert.

Although I have heard its gulping nighttime calls, which seem to emanate from a prehistoric creature in the depths of an impenetrable swamp and have earned it the nicknames thunder pumper, stake driver, and bog bull, I have yet to see another American bittern. Recently, however, on a visit to Cardinal Marsh near Decorah, Iowa, I saw two small birds fly by, flashing buffy wing coverts, and land in the marsh grasses, where they stood motionless with bills pointed toward the sky. They had to be least bitterns, the only other bittern in North America, one of the smallest herons worldwide, and a life bird for me.

Unlike most other herons, the American bittern, which ornithologist Arthur Cleveland Bent called a "recluse of the marshes" and a "shy denizen of the swamps," is primarily a solitary bird. It favors large freshwater wetlands with tall vegetation and some open shallow water, where it can wait patiently at the water's edge or step slowly and silently until it captures a fish or other aquatic creature with a sudden thrust of its bill.

Breeding occurs in any suitable habitat across most of the United States and Canada. The male booms to defend his territory. In courtship he shortens his neck, lowers his abdomen, and expands the white patches on his back. Mates engage in aerial displays. The female builds a nest of sticks, grass, and sedge in dense marsh growth or grasses on dry ground near water; she incubates her eggs for about four weeks and apparently cares for her three to five young alone. When she returns to the nest with partially digested food, a nestling will grab and hold on to her bill until she regurgitates food into its mouth. She feeds her babies for one to two weeks in the nest and for about two more weeks after they leave it. Age of first flight is about seven or eight weeks. During migration and on its wintering grounds in coastal waters, this species continues its solitary habits.

Although widely distributed across the country, the American bittern has never been abundant. Now it is undergoing a substantial decline, especially in the southern part of its range, due to loss and degradation of wetland habitat from chemical contamination, acid rain, and human development.

Yellow-crowned night-heron (above)
and black-crowned night-heron

Black-crowned and Yellow-crowned Night-Herons

Nycticorax nycticorax and *Nyctanassa violacea*

I saw my first black-crowned night-heron in Loring Park near downtown Minneapolis. This species occurs across the country and on every continent except Australia and Antarctica. It is more gregarious and occupies a wider variety of aquatic habitats than does the yellow-crowned night-heron. The yellow-crown occurs in cypress swamps, mangroves, and bayous and along lowland rivers with heavy cover mostly in the southeastern and south central states but also up the Atlantic Coast and the Mississippi River.

Black-crowns are summer residents in Minnesota. In recent years, there have been few reports of yellow-crowns, once regular visitors to the state. Because they are most active at night both herons are difficult to see, which may make them seem less common than they are. However, they are sometimes visible by day, especially during breeding season.

The black-crown eats mostly fish plus other aquatic animals, rodents, eggs, baby birds, and carrion. Its cousin uses its exceptionally stout bill to feed primarily on crustaceans such as crabs and crayfish. It also eats frogs, insects, and fish.

In 2005 the discovery of eight yellow-crowns in Lucas County generated excitement among Iowa birders. Aaron Brees of Des Moines assumed they were present due to a pool that was losing water, thus concentrating prey. He wrote, "Without a situation like this to bring these birds to a spot that is visible to us, we usually don't get anywhere near good spots for them." Because of the inaccessibility of their usual habitat, he speculated that breeding regularly takes place undiscovered in this marshy region.

Yellow-crowns breed in isolated pairs or small groups. In display, the male stretches his neck, points his bill up, crouches with plumes erect, and squawks. Pairs touch bills and nibble each other's feathers. Black-crowns nest in colonies. The male chooses a nest site from which he displays for potential mates by ruffing his feathers with neck up and forward. He also bows and raises his feet alternately while giving a hissing buzz.

The two species are similar in that both sexes participate in building platform nests of sticks in trees or shrubs. Both parents incubate the eggs and feed their young, which are able to fly at about six weeks of age. Northern populations winter in Central or South America; southern birds are permanent residents. Threats include loss of wetlands, water pollution, and pesticides.

I am still waiting to see my first yellow-crowned night-heron. Meanwhile, I find pleasure in reports from other birders and am hopeful that the enthusiasm created by sightings of this species will translate into advocacy for habitat preservation.

White-faced Ibis

Plegadis chihi

On April 20, 2005, I visited Cardinal Marsh in northeast Iowa with my friends Carol and Fred. On our arrival, we heard the creaking notes of yellow-headed blackbirds and the whinny of a pied-billed grebe. Then on an island in one of the ponds, we noticed a heron-like bird with glossy chestnut and greenish feathers and a long, decurved bill. I had never seen this species, but Carol and Fred knew immediately that it was an ibis. The white border around its red facial skin meant that the bird was a white-faced ibis in breeding plumage. Nonbreeding birds do not have this marking and are almost impossible to distinguish from the glossy ibis, the only other North American bird of the genus *Plegadis*.

Ibises are in a family with spoonbills, which are similar in shape but have spatula-tipped bills. Most species in this family occur only in the tropics. In the United States, the glossy ibis is an eastern bird, while the white-face occurs mainly west of the Mississippi River, where it forages for insects, crustaceans, and earthworms in freshwater marshes, irrigated land, damp meadows, or salt marshes. It finds prey by touch while probing in mud with its sensitive bill.

Migratory white-faced ibises breed sporadically in the western states as far east as North and South Dakota. Wintering grounds extend as far south as northern South America and include the coastal areas of California, Texas, and Louisiana, where white-faces are also permanent residents. In spring males arrive on the breeding grounds first and defend small territories within a large colony. Mates form pair bonds by preening each other, rubbing their heads together, and entwining their necks. The male gathers plant material and the female builds a platform nest in dense marsh vegetation. They take turns sitting on their three or four eggs for about three weeks. Young birds feed by sticking their heads into either parent's mouth and receiving partially digested food. They are able to fly skillfully about five weeks after hatching.

Plegadis ibises wander widely, a trait that has aided expansion of their normal ranges. An increase of sightings in Minnesota has led to the speculation that the white-faced ibis may soon be regarded as a regular species instead of a casual or rare visitor to the state.

Although populations have increased since the banning of DDT in the United States and Canada, the use of DDT in Mexico continues to cause eggshell thinning even among birds that migrate north to breed. The greatest concern for these birds, however, is human encroachment on suitable wetlands.

I am grateful for the preservation of Cardinal Marsh, clearly a suitable wetland not only for the white-faced ibis but for other species as well. This area has never disappointed me in my search for birds, and I don't expect that it ever will.

Osprey

Pandion haliaetus

Perched on top of a utility pole holding a fat, foot-long fish in its talons was a bird of prey my husband and I had never seen. Its white head with a dark crown and eye stripes and white underparts contrasted sharply with its brown back. We soon identified the bird as an osprey or fish hawk. Although we have since seen this species flying over the Mississippi River and the Root River near our home, our first sighting at Point Reyes National Seashore in California remains the most vivid in our minds.

In flight, the osprey carries its long, narrow wings angled and bowed down. At its most dramatic, the bird hovers over water, then folds its wings and dives headfirst until, just before hitting the water, it throws its feet forward to catch a fish in its talons. Specialized barbed pads on its feet help to grip the slippery fish. Because this species is so specialized, the American Ornithologists' Union places it in its own subfamily of hawks.

Breeding generally occurs across the northern states and Canada. Some ospreys breed on the southern coasts, where they are permanent residents. Birds from the Midwest winter in South America. Young birds stay south until they are two or three years old, when they return north for their first nesting attempts. Most don't successfully breed until the age of five.

Ospreys usually mate for life. Prior to nesting, mates engage in aerial displays. The bulky stick nest is built by both sexes at the top of a large tree near water. Other tall structures, such as utility poles or artificial platforms, are also common sites. A pair may reuse a nest for years, adding material each year, until the nest threatens to collapse its supporting structure. The female, with assistance from her mate, incubates their three or four eggs for about five weeks. At first she remains with the chicks while the father brings fish for her to feed them; later, she also hunts. Fledging occurs in about seven to eight weeks. Because this species migrates individually, the juveniles must be fully independent by fall.

At one time these hawks nested more broadly across the country, but in the mid 1900s DDT and other pesticides began taking a serious toll. Since the banning of DDT, they have recovered somewhat, partly due to reintroduction efforts, placement of artificial nest platforms, and habitat improvement. In the Twin Cities area of Minnesota, reintroduction began in 1984. By 2003, thirty-seven nest sites in the area had fledged two hundred seventy chicks. In Wisconsin, the osprey has recovered from eighty-two nests statewide in 1974 to more than four hundred nests in 2005. Recovery efforts are sure to continue because osprey fans are intensely involved in the welfare of "their" birds and keep watch over the entire breeding process.

Red-shouldered Hawk

Buteo lineatus

When not in use for nesting, our bluebird house has provided a perch for various birds. One year in March a red-shouldered hawk perched there, displaying its orange shoulders and the orange barring on its breast and belly. Later that summer I heard the *keeyuur* call of this species, but it seemed different and I thought maybe a blue jay was imitating the hawk. Soon I saw two juvenile hawks vocalizing and interacting as they flew along the edge of the woods. This activity continued intermittently for several days.

Except for the fact that red-shouldered hawks are uncommon, I shouldn't have been surprised at the appearance of these birds in their typical woodland habitat. Unlike other buteos, the red-shoulder is able to navigate skillfully among trees with a flapping then gliding flight pattern, similar to that of accipiters such as the sharp-shinned hawk. Like the accipiters, it preys chiefly on small birds, although it also preys on small mammals, amphibians, and reptiles.

Most red-shouldered hawks breed in deciduous woods, often near rivers and swamps, from eastern Minnesota south to Texas and east to the Atlantic Coast. Breeding also occurs in western California. Displays include vocalizing while flapping, swooping, diving, or circling high over territories. Both sexes build a platform nest of sticks lined with softer material commonly thirty-five to sixty-five feet high, close to the trunk of a deciduous tree. As with other hawks, the female does most of the incubating with her mate occasionally taking a turn while she eats the food he has brought her. For the first few weeks after hatching, the mother stays with the three or four nestlings and feeds them food brought by the male. After the young fledge at around six weeks of age, the parents continue to feed them for approximately two more months.

Although red-shouldered hawks may migrate as far as central Mexico for the winter, most are short-distance migrants or permanent residents. I have seen this species in January in the Whitewater Wildlife Management Area in southeast Minnesota.

Once among the most common hawks of the eastern states, red-shoulder populations dropped considerably throughout the twentieth century. Pesticides are partly to blame, but habitat loss due to fragmentation of forests is even more troublesome. The bird is presently listed as endangered in Iowa and Illinois, threatened in Wisconsin and Michigan, and a species of special concern in Minnesota.

Because of the juveniles present in my area, I suspected a nest was nearby, but I didn't find one. I don't often hear or see these birds, so I am happy whenever a *keeyuur* call reaches my ears, and I hope that one day another red-shouldered hawk will find our bluebird house a convenient place to perch.

Swainson's Hawk

Buteo swainsoni

Binoculars held ready, Doc forges ahead across a field to the edge of a woodlot. It is April 16, 1988, and members of our fledgling Fillmore County Birders club are exploring an area that was once prairie in the western part of the county. Our leaders are Mary Jo and Gordon Dathe from nearby Spring Valley. Dr. Alden Risser is our most seasoned birder. When we catch up with him, we spot a large nest above us in a tree. Doc identifies the occupant as a Swainson's hawk.

John Hockema, one of Doc's protégés and now an expert birder himself, has returned to that place every spring since 1988. Fifteen years in a row, he found Swainson's hawks nesting there. Then, in 2003, to his dismay, he found a development had replaced the woodlot. He didn't see the birds that year or the next, but in 2005, although he couldn't find a nest, he saw one Swainson's circling overhead. Suddenly he found himself waving to the bird as if to an old friend.

Although it occasionally strays into eastern states, this species is primarily a bird of the Great Plains. By soaring high and low over arid and semi-arid country or perching on a fence post or the ground, it hunts for small mammals, reptiles, and large insects. In courtship mates engage in circling flights and deep dives. The nest is a platform of sticks lined with fresh leaves, flower clusters, down, and feathers in a tree or large shrub fifteen to thirty feet above ground. The male brings food to his mate while she sits on her eggs; later, he brings food for her to feed the nestlings. The young are able to fly about six weeks after hatching but may remain with their parents until fall migration.

Unlike red-shouldered hawks, these birds are long-distance migrants, traveling five to seven thousand miles in large swirling flocks to the pampas of Argentina for the winter. In the first half of the twentieth century, flocks contained many thousands of birds, but that number has since declined and the Swainson's hawk is now listed federally as a species of special concern. Major problems are habitat destruction and the increased use of pesticides related to agricultural expansion in Argentina and along a narrow migration corridor in Veracruz, Mexico, through which most Swainson's hawks pass. The birds are also sensitive to human disturbance, which frequently results in nest desertion.

Two years ago, thanks to directions from Minnesota birder Craig Mandel, I found a Swainson's hawk soaring over farm fields about twenty miles west of my home. Although I hadn't seen this species in many years, I recognized its chestnut bib, rocking motion in flight, and long, tapered wings reaching up into a medium that we can navigate only in machines.

Golden Eagle

Aquila chrysaetos

Golden eagles often appear next to bald eagles in field guides but are genetically closer to buteos such as red-tailed hawks. In the Upper Midwest, along the Mississippi River, it is possible to see dozens of bald eagles a day in fall and winter. The golden eagle, named for its golden crown and nape, is most common in open mountains, foothills, and plains from the Dakotas to the West Coast. It is also present on similar terrain in Europe and Asia.

Both species reach maturity at about four years of age. Because goldens, particularly after their first year, may look very similar to immature balds, misidentification is common. Despite opportunities to observe goldens with people who are more adept than I am, I lack the confidence to identify this bird on my own. A sighting of a golden eagle that was especially helpful occurred in 2003 on Fred Lesher's annual field trip between La Crosse, Wisconsin, and Lansing, Iowa. While the bird leisurely circled above us, Jeff Dankert, a raptor expert from Winona, pointed out diagnostic characteristics—a relatively small head and long tail, large white patches on the flight feathers instead of diffused white areas as in the bald, curvature of the wings as opposed to the straight broad wings of the bald, and the moderate dihedral position of the wings in flight. After this instruction, I felt sure that I could identify this species, but the next eagle in question found me doubting myself again.

Habitat and behavior also offer clues to identification. Unlike the bald, the golden eagle usually appears away from water, hunts more than it scavenges, and generally preys not on fish but on mammals such as ground squirrels and jackrabbits. It often flies below the tree line and hugs contours of ridges that shield it from potential prey.

Golden eagles form long-term pair bonds. Aerial displays are common in courtship. Large stick nests, constructed by both sexes, are usually built on cliff edges; the birds may maintain and enlarge two or more nests that they use in different years. The female does more incubating than her mate and remains with her two young most of the time at first, while the male hunts. Before fledging at about nine weeks of age, young birds exercise their great wings while hopping around on surrounding branches. By fall, birds that breed and hatch farthest north are on their way to Mexico for the winter. Others are permanent residents or short-distance migrants.

In 1962 golden eagles were added to the Federal Bald Eagle Protection Act in response to ranchers' habit of destroying thousands of these birds despite little evidence of livestock depredation. Current populations are below historical highs but appear to be stable. Present dangers include human disturbance near nests and poison intended for other animals such as coyotes.

Peregrine Falcon

Falco peregrinus

When I entered his room, I couldn't resist exclaiming about the peregrine falcon speeding past his window, although I knew my leukemia patient was unlikely to take his eyes off the large syringe in my hand. Hoping to provide distraction as I slowly injected the chemotherapy, I told him about the peregrines raising four babies in a nest box on the Mayo Clinic building across the street. I told him that the falcons, once nearly extinct due to pesticide-induced reproductive failures, have returned to their historical habitation in the Midwest thanks to the banning of DDT and reintroduction efforts. After that day, my patient often watched the birds from his hospital window.

Peregrines breed in much of Canada, along our western coast and in other western states, along parts of the East Coast, and increasingly in the Midwest. Their return to Minnesota is largely due to Bud Tordoff, professor emeritus of the Department of Ecology, Evolution, and Behavior at the University of Minnesota, who coordinated reintroduction into the state and continues to monitor the birds. The Raptor Resource Project, founded by falconer Bob Anderson, and the Iowa Peregrine Falcon Recovery Team are responsible for bringing the falcon back to Iowa. Recovery programs also operate in other midwestern states.

Every spring peregrines strengthen their long-term pair bonds with courtship feeding and vocalizing during high circling flights, dives, and chases. Nests are usually simple scrapes on cliff edges in open country, but the birds also nest in boxes placed for them on ledges of buildings. Power companies interested in good public relations prefer to host peregrines on their smokestacks rather than to poison nuisance pigeons, a favored prey of the falcons. During Fred Lesher's spring Mississippi River trips, we always stop to watch the peregrines at the power plant in Genoa, Wisconsin.

Incubation of a pair's three to four eggs is mostly by the female, whose mate brings pigeons and other birds to her on the nest. The young hatch in about a month and fledge about six weeks later. As with other raptors, for the first couple of weeks the father brings prey for the mother to tear apart for their babies. In fall, young birds hatched in the north will begin their first long-distance migration to Central or South America. Those in more temperate climates are usually permanent residents.

Despite being a fierce predator, this species has for centuries been the most popular bird among falconers because of its gentle behavior with humans and capacity to be trained. Its regal appearance and spectacular flying ability have also contributed to its popularity. One of the most breathtaking sights in the avian world is that of a peregrine diving at a speed of up to two hundred miles an hour to capture a bird in midair.

Sora (above) and yellow rail

Sora

Porzana carolina

One spring, while visiting my neighbor Phil Rutter, I noticed many small birds in his fallow fields and hazelnut plantings. There I saw bluebirds, bobolinks, meadowlarks, and the endangered Henslow's sparrow. Then I saw a chickenlike bird walking around his farm pond. It was a sora. I had heard the diagnostic descending whinny of this rail before but had never had a good view of it because it was usually hidden in marsh grasses.

Four species of rails occur in the Upper Midwest—sora, yellow, king, and Virginia. All are small to medium-size, short-tailed, stubby-winged birds that are mostly solitary and frequently active at night. Their laterally compressed bodies, giving rise to the term "thin as a rail," and their cryptic plumage allow them to move invisibly between marsh grasses, thus avoiding predators. Of all these species, the sora is the one that birders most frequently see, as it occasionally walks around in full view at the edge of a pond picking up seeds, insects, and snails from the ground or probing in mud with its bill. Generally, however, loud vocalizations in defense of territories are the only indications of a rail's presence.

Soras breed in freshwater marshes across the country except in the Southeast but often winter in saltwater habitat along our southern coasts and in Central and South America. In courtship, mates engage in mutual preening, bowing and facing toward then away from each other. Both sexes build the nest, which is a basket of aquatic vegetation supported by surrounding stems just above water, sometimes with vegetation arching over it and a path of plant material leading to the entrance. The female lays five to twelve eggs, which is typical of North American rails. Incubation by both parents begins as soon as the first few eggs are laid; thus the chicks do not all hatch at the same time. One parent may care for young already out of the nest, while the other incubates the remaining eggs. Young birds are able to fly at about three weeks of age.

All North American rails have declined in recent decades because of diminishing wetland habitat. In the late 1800s, Johan Hvoslef recorded the four Upper Midwest species in Fillmore County. Now, in Minnesota, the king is endangered and the yellow, which has a localized presence in the northwestern part of the state, is a species of special concern. I asked three expert birders, longtime Iowa birder Dennis Carter, Luther College ornithologist Tex Sordahl, and Fred Lesher, which rails they have seen in our area. All three have seen soras and Virginias, but only Fred has found a king, which he saw about thirty years ago near La Crosse, and a yellow, which he once heard at the Trempealeau National Wildlife Refuge.

Common Moorhen

Gallinula chloropus

When my husband and I arrived at Cardinal Marsh on July 21, 2006, we found a marsh wren fussing in the brush, two sandhill cranes trumpeting in the distance, and pied-billed grebes floating in the water, diving, and reappearing in different places. We were hoping to find the two families of common moorhens that Dennis Carter and others had observed on July 4. When I walked down to the water for a closer look, I heard a sora calling and thought I saw it walking along the edge of the pond. We frequently hear soras but don't often see them, so I quickly pointed out the bird to my husband. He immediately noticed its bright red bill and facial shield. Because a sora has a bright yellow bill, we soon realized, to our delight, that the bird we were watching could be none other than a common moorhen, only the second time we had ever seen this species.

For more than an hour we observed the moorhen as it foraged in plain sight. Although we never saw the other adults and young birds that Dennis had reported, our intense observation of the marsh grasses eventually yielded the sighting of two adult and one juvenile least bitterns, a rare experience for us.

Moorhens are in the same family as rails but look more like ducks and are not as secretive as rails. They forage for aquatic vegetation, berries, insects, and snails in the manner of rails by walking on land or stepping through marsh grasses, but they also forage by swimming, like their relatives the American coots, with which they often associate.

As with other Rallidae, moorhens communicate primarily by vocalizations, especially when forming breeding territories. In describing their calls, the 1917 book *Birds of America* anthropomorphizes in a way that is unacceptable today but which I find charming: "There is the appealing *ticket, ticket* of the lovelorn male, the petulant *tuka, tuka* of despondency, and the questioning explosive *chuck* of inquiry."

Courtship involves chases, mutual preening of feathers, bowing, and exposing white undertail patches. The nest is a platform of aquatic plants with a ramp leading down to water. Both sexes build the nest and incubate their eight to eleven eggs for about three weeks. The young can swim soon after hatching and are able to find most of their own food within three weeks. Before then, they are fed by their parents and sometimes by siblings from an earlier brood.

According to Thomas S. Roberts in *The Birds of Minnesota*, moorhens were once common across southern Minnesota. Now they are a state species of special concern and occur only in the southeastern corner. They are more common in states farther east and south and are present on other continents, but wetland loss has caused a decline in all populations.

Whooping Crane

Grus americana

"Get out of the car, people!" yelled normally soft-spoken Fred Lesher. Fred, Carol Schumacher, and I were searching for two whooping crane sisters who had wandered away from their flock in Wisconsin to a marsh near New Albin, Iowa. After scanning the marsh repeatedly without success, Carol and I put our scopes away and climbed back into the car. Fred, however, scanned the area once more and suddenly spotted the sisters in the distance. For a better look we drove down a dirt trail and found the cranes, North America's tallest birds, nearly in full view, showing their red crowns, red cheeks, magnificent white bodies, and great white bustles.

Although opportunities to see whooping cranes in the wild are rare, chances are better than they once were. By 1941, hunting and wetland loss had reduced the world's only population of this species to just sixteen. By February 2005, thanks to reintroduction and conservation efforts, the number had climbed to four hundred fifty-nine.

The only natural flock breeds in Wood Buffalo National Park in northwest Canada and winters in Aransas National Wildlife Refuge in Texas. Another flock begins life in captivity at Patuxent Wildlife Research Center in Maryland, where each year a class of young cranes is imprinted on ultralight aircraft by handlers who broadcast crane calls, wear white costumes, and use crane puppets to interact with the birds. The chicks are then sent to Necedah National Wildlife Refuge in Wisconsin to prepare for fall migration behind an ultralight plane to Chassahowitzka National Wildlife Refuge in Florida. Since the project's inception in 2001, most of the birds have returned to Wisconsin on their own and continue to migrate without assistance. A third, nonmigratory flock in Florida has also had success. Because these birds occur in limited concentrations, a primary concern is that disease, a natural disaster, or an oil spill could decimate a whole flock.

It is good to know that whooping cranes still exist and continue to engage in their natural life cycles, including the elaborate courtship dances that involve leaping, head bobbing, grass tossing, bowing, and whooping. The nest, built on the ground by both sexes, is a mound of vegetation with a depression in the center. Both parents incubate the two eggs for about a month and then feed their young a variety of aquatic animals and vegetation. In the wild, usually only one chick survives, but in captivity, where food is sufficient, both chicks generally live.

Young birds leave the nest soon after hatching and are able to fly about three months later. In fall, they will by nature join their parents, following traditional migration corridors to wintering grounds in Texas. By human design, they will be among the young birds following an ultralight plane on their first trip to Florida.

Upland Sandpiper

Bartramia longicauda

Its cryptic plumage blending with the surrounding grass made the bird almost invisible to normal eyes, but not to the eyes of John Hockema, who had promised to show the Fillmore County Birders an upland sandpiper near his grandmother's farm. John told us the bird was standing on a small rise. Soon we could see its head against the sky, and finally we could distinguish the whole sandpiper. Although a true shorebird in appearance and in some of its behavior, this species rarely frequents shores but spends its time on prairies, open meadows, and fields, and increasingly, due to the absence of its preferred habitat, near airports. It forages by walking through fields with jerky movements and picking up insects, earthworms, snails, and seeds from the ground or from vegetation.

Breeding grounds are in open country across the northern states from the East Coast to the Great Plains and into northwest Canada. While displaying high above the ground with shallow, fluttering wingbeats, the male sings an eerie bubbling and whistling song. Nesting often takes place in loose colonies with egg laying and hatching occurring in synchrony among all the pairs. The nest, probably built by both sexes, is a shallow scrape on the ground in dense vegetation with grass arching over it. The female usually lays four eggs, which she and her mate incubate for three to four weeks. Young birds leave the nest within hours after hatching and are able to feed themselves, although their parents remain close and perform distraction displays when predators approach. First flights take place about a month after hatching, and by fall the juveniles are ready for their long migration to wintering grounds in Argentina, Brazil, and Chile.

Upland sandpipers have had an uneven history. In the early 1800s numbers increased with the clearing of eastern forests. Then in the late 1800s, commercial hunting led to a dramatic drop in population. In 1932 Thomas S. Roberts wrote that this bird was once "present all through the summer everywhere in the open country in countless thousands." With federal protection through the Migratory Bird Treaty Act of 1918, numbers gradually began to rise, but Roberts still questioned "whether the remnant left can be saved even with careful protection."

Although recovery continued for some time, this species never returned to its former abundance and at present is declining again due to reemergence of woodlands in abandoned fields and loss of grasslands. In addition, early mowing of hay fields destroys a significant number of nests. Only in the Great Plains are numbers apparently stable. John Hockema recently told me that in Minnesota he has seen small groups of the sandpipers in one area for several years, then they have disappeared, and he has found another group elsewhere. However, as time passes, even these groups are dwindling.

Wilson's Phalarope

Phalaropus tricolor

The bird was swimming on a pond in the Whitewater Wildlife Management Area in southeast Minnesota. It had a long, thin bill like most sandpipers, but I had never seen a sandpiper swimming before. When it began spinning around, I remembered reading about phalaropes and their habit of spinning to stir up aquatic organisms, which they then catch with quick stabbing motions. Their ability to swim comes from their lobed and partially webbed toes, characteristics that other sandpipers do not have. However, like their relatives, phalaropes may also forage for insects and other invertebrates by walking along shores and poking their bills into mud. I quickly consulted my field guide and identified the bird in the pond as a Wilson's phalarope.

This species inhabits prairie lakes, freshwater marshes, and mudflats but in winter may also inhabit salty water. It breeds across the northern Great Plains into western Minnesota. The other two birds in this genus, the red-necked and red phalarope, breed in the Arctic and are strongly pelagic, spending most of the year feeding in oceans.

The most notable trait of phalaropes is their reversal of sexual attributes. Like her relatives, the Wilson's female is larger and has more colorful breeding plumage than the male. In courtship, she competes for males by chasing them, stretching her neck, and fluffing her neck feathers. She may have more than one mate. Nests, started by the female but finished by her mates, are shallow depressions lined with grass on the ground near water. After laying four eggs in each nest, the female's work is done. The males then incubate the eggs for about three weeks. Chicks are able to move about and feed themselves within a day of hatching, while their fathers watch over them and distract predators by feigning injury.

In fall, Wilson's gather at salty or alkaline lakes like California's Mono Lake and Utah's Great Salt Lake before migrating to their wintering grounds in South America. The other two phalaropes migrate offshore to spend the winter in southern oceans. Occasionally, however, the red-neck, which I have observed twice, also migrates inland. On May 13, 2000, my neighbor, Phil Rutter, invited me to see four of these birds that were present on his farm pond; on August 12, 2006, at Cardinal Marsh, Iowa birder Marian Miller and I identified a red-neck busily swimming and jabbing at the water with its needlelike bill.

In 2006 reports of the red-neck in the Upper Midwest equaled and possibly exceeded those of the Wilson's, which has been in decline since 1982 and is now on Minnesota's threatened species list and the Audubon WatchList for species of conservation concern. Problems include the draining of prairie wetlands and the diversion of water from major staging areas, which changes the ecology of hypersaline lakes.

Snowy Owl

Bubo scandiacus

On Highway 43 between Rushford and Winona, Minnesota, the slanted tops of utility poles create optical illusions of perching birds. In December 1996, while driving home after a day of birding with Carol Schumacher, I noticed something white, perhaps a play of light, on top of a pole near the little settlement of Hart. I continued driving, then turned around. No one else needed to know that the poles had tricked me again. What I found, however, was not an illusion, although it was an apparition of sorts, still as a statue, a round-headed ghost in the dusk, a snowy owl. Camouflaged for northern winters, the bird was pure white except for its eyes, beak, and sparse dark bars across its breast and back, meaning that it was probably an adult male; females and immatures generally have more streaking.

Snowy owls are large, powerful birds that breed in the high Arctic tundra, where lemmings are their preferred food. Nests and concentrations of owls occur in places where lemmings are abundant; in years when there are no such places, the owls may not breed at all. In early spring the male defends his territory with great bellowing hoots. To strengthen their lifelong bond, he bows before his mate, fluffs his feathers, and dances stiffly, often with a lemming in his mouth. The female lays her eggs in a simple depression on a raised site with good visibility. The clutch size of three to eleven eggs varies according to the abundance of prey. Hunting day and night, watching for prey from a perch or while flying low and hovering, the male brings food to his incubating mate and later brings food for her to feed the nestlings. Fledging occurs at one to three weeks of age, but young birds are not efficient fliers until about seven weeks after hatching. Their parents feed them until they are about ten weeks old.

In winter, the owls may move south to inhabit dunes, beaches, prairies, and fields throughout Canada and just inside our northern border from Minnesota to the East Coast. Movement relates to the availability of food, which can become sparse due to an overpopulation of owls, a precipitous decline in lemmings, or unusually deep or crusty snow. When lemmings are unavailable, prey items increase to include rabbits, hares, birds, and fish. Occasionally the owls take animals from traps or seize grouse and ptarmigans before the hunters who have shot them arrive at the site.

The sparser the food, the farther south snowies migrate. When they reach as far as southern Minnesota, they are often starving, which was particularly true during an unusually early winter irruption in 2005. Whenever I see these magnificent creatures from the Arctic in my area, I am aware that my opportunity comes at a hard time for the birds.

Northern Hawk Owl

Surnia ulula

We found the owl perched high in a tree, slowly turning its warriorlike head and preening its feathers, apparently oblivious to the people watching it from below. The bird looked different from any owl I had ever seen, a little like a hawk in the shape of its head and its long tail. However, its face, rimmed by black semicircles, was distinctly owl. Unruffled behavior when humans are present is not unusual for this species. What was unusual, however, was the bird's location in the small town of Manly in north central Iowa.

Hawk owls live primarily on the edges of spruce and tamarack forests in Canada and Alaska, where they watch and listen for prey while perching on the tops of coniferous trees or, like sharp-shinned hawks, while maneuvering skillfully through brushy cover and hovering in midair. Another hawklike characteristic is their habit of hunting during the day. Excellent vision, acute hearing, and swift flight allow these owls to locate and capture prey with inordinate accuracy. Rodents, particularly voles, are their preferred food. The number of eggs a female lays, anywhere from four to nine, relates to the abundance of this food.

In courtship, mates sing whistling duets. The male bows stiffly, feeds his mate, and stores prey near the nest, which is in the hollow stub of a tree, a large tree cavity, or the abandoned nest of a crow or hawk. The female sits on her eggs for approximately a month and stays with her young for the first couple of weeks, while the male brings food. Before fledging, about five weeks after hatching, the young climb about in the nest tree flapping their wings.

The juvenile birds will be hunting on their own by winter, eating rodents, ptarmigans, sharp-tailed grouse, and small birds. When food is scarce, these normally nonmigratory owls move south. During the winter of 2004–05, northern Minnesota saw a huge irruption of Canadian and Alaskan owls, including hawk, great gray, and boreal owls, which led to an invasion of birdwatchers from across the country. Apparently, conditions were better in the high Arctic, as snowy owls arrived in lesser numbers.

Sadly for me, a back injury precluded the long trip to Duluth, but compensation came when the hawk owl appeared in Iowa, much farther south than these birds usually travel even in invasion years. I could manage that relatively short trip, so on February 22 I accompanied three friends to Manly, where we quickly found the bird. To make the most out of this single sighting, I studied the owl for a long time through a spotting scope. When I looked deep into its yellow eyes, it seemed as if the visitor from the North was looking directly back at me and we were the only creatures that existed.

Great Gray Owl

Strix nebulosa

Most of the great gray owls in North America inhabit the coniferous forests, meadows, and bogs in Canada and Alaska, where meadow voles are their primary source of food. Every few years, according to Canadian conservation biologist and great gray expert Jim Duncan, the vole population plummets and the owls move south of their normal range to prey on small birds and a variety of small mammals. Typically, northern Minnesota sees about thirty-five great grays a year. The huge winter invasion of 2004–05 yielded more than four thousand five hundred sightings, ten times the previous record. Because of the birds' affinity for roadsides, where utility poles and signs offered good opportunities for perching and viewing prey, birders were able to see as many as twenty owls a day. However, the busy highways proved deadly for many of these birds; more died from collisions with cars than from hunger.

Great grays are only a little larger than barred owls, which they resemble, but their dense plumage makes them appear much bigger. Broad, round facial disks help funnel sounds to their slightly asymmetrical ears, which aid in pinpointing prey in as much as a foot of snow. In powerful dives, the birds can break snow crust thick enough to hold humans and capture prey with their exceptionally sharp talons. Excellent day and night vision allows for observation of movement through grass or snow more than a hundred yards away. Although this species generally hunts from low perches in open country, breeding takes place in dense forests.

In courtship the male engages in aerial displays and feeds the female. Mates preen each other's feathers. Depending on the abundance of voles, the female lays two to five eggs, usually in the abandoned nest of another large bird. She incubates the eggs for about a month and broods her newly hatched babies for a couple of weeks, during which time her mate provides food. Soon the young birds are able to hop around outside the nest. By the end of September, they are flying well and hunting on their own.

On March 4, 2005, I heard Jim Duncan speak during the festival of owls organized by Karla Kinstler at the Houston Nature Center in southeast Minnesota. That evening, word was spreading of a great gray that had wandered farther south than usual to nearby Winona County. Over the next few weeks many people saw the bird, including my husband and me. While watching the owl perched on a fence post, its feathers ruffling in the wind, we could clearly see its yellow eyes and white bow tie. Soon it dove for prey and missed, then moved across the road to another fence post. Not wanting to disturb the first great gray we had ever seen, we soon left, wishing it well.

Northern Saw-whet Owl

Aegolius acadicus

Smaller than a robin, the saw-whet is difficult to see because of its size, nocturnal habits, and plumage that looks like its surroundings. My friend Karla Kinstler knows something not only of saw-whets but also of all the owls in our region. Her interest in owls began when Alice, a great horned owl with a damaged wing, came to live with her and taught her many intricacies of owl behavior. Although she has never seen a saw-whet in her area, Karla usually hears them in late winter near her house.

To defend his territory and attract a mate, the male toots a rhythmic *sweee-awwww* throughout late winter nights. He circles a potential mate, bobs before her, and may offer her a mouse or insect. If she accepts, copulation soon occurs. The female lays five or six eggs in an abandoned woodpecker hole or artificial nest box. She sits on her eggs for about a month, then broods her nestlings for three weeks, while her mate provides food in the form of deer mice, other small rodents, small birds, and large insects that he locates with the aid of his excellent vision and remarkable hearing. Nature has afforded this little bird its astounding capacity to hear by giving it huge asymmetrical ear cavities. Differences in loudness and the time it takes sound to reach each ear allow him to pinpoint the direction and distance of prey. The mother may also hunt for the young when they leave the nest at about four weeks, or she will begin a second brood with another mate, while the father cares for their fledglings.

Saw-whets breed and winter in coniferous or mixed coniferous forests across the lower half of Canada and much of this country except southern states from Texas to the East Coast. Some birds move south in severe winters. Populations have recently declined slightly, due in part to loss of habitat.

Considering the difficulty of seeing a saw-whet, the presence of one, discovered by droppings along the trunk of its roosting tree during the late nineties in southeast Minnesota, attracted the attention of many birders. Karla described her encounter with the bird in February 1999: "My first experience with a wild saw-whet owl was the nearly legendary owl of Wiscoy Valley. As advertised, the owl was perched at eye level just above some poopsicles in a small pine tree. It wasn't the slightest bit concerned as I approached to within six feet, or when I kept slipping on the ice-covered snow and falling on my butt while trying to photograph it! It hardly even opened an eye at my disturbance." The unruffled behavior of saw-whets and other owls in the presence of people may be due in part to the security of their camouflaging plumage and habits of inactivity during daylight hours.

Red-headed Woodpecker

Melanerpes erythrocephalus

"That was a red-headed woodpecker!" I exclaimed. My nephew Kevin, who was in the car with me, said, "How did you know that? I hardly saw it." I had to think for a moment about how I identify birds, an almost unconscious act for me. I have learned to note in an instant a bird's size, shape, markings, vocalizations, flight pattern, behavior, and habitat and then pay attention to my gut feeling for a quick identification. The red-headed woodpecker, however, is easy for anyone to recognize because of its striking plumage— white underparts, rump, and wing patches that contrast with its blue-black back and bright red head.

Across the eastern half of the country to the edge of the Great Plains, this woodpecker inhabits open areas with large scattered trees, especially oak and beech. It has the same short legs, strong claws, stiff tail, and chisel-shaped bill as other woodpeckers, which allow it to climb trees and drill for insects and sap. More often than other woodpeckers, the red-head flies out from perches to catch insects in midair. It also comes to feeders for suet and sunflower seeds. Nuts gathered in fall are stored for winter in holes and crevices.

In winter northern birds usually migrate to the Southeast, while southern birds are permanent residents. Birds that do not migrate may use a male's winter territory as the breeding territory and his winter roosting cavity in a dead tree or utility pole as the nest site. Males advertise their territories with calling and drumming. Aggressive displays include bobbing, wing spreading, and tail spreading. In courtship mates chase each other and bob around opposite sides of tree stubs or utility poles. When a pair creates a new nest cavity, the male does most of the excavating and the female shows acceptance by tapping on the site. Both sexes incubate the four to five eggs for about two weeks and feed their nestlings, who fledge about one month after hatching. After fledging, young birds remain with their parents for about twenty-five days or until the adults begin to raise a second brood.

Red-headed woodpeckers are on the Audubon WatchList of conservation concern. Throughout their range they have declined by fifty percent over the last forty years. Reasons for the decline are not clear. Some dangers include collisions with cars when birds fly out to catch insects along roadsides; failure of nests in utility poles that have been treated with creosote; and habitat degradation related to clearcuts, the harvesting of snags, regeneration of forests, and fire suppression.

I exclaimed over the red-headed woodpecker I saw with Kevin because these birds, which used to be regular visitors to our feeders, are now difficult to find. For just an occasional glimpse of one, I have to look carefully in open country with some large trees.

Acadian Flycatcher

Empidonax virescens

Beaver Creek, a jewel of clear water tripping over rocks and brilliant green watercress, winds through the state park of the same name in southeastern Minnesota. It is May 31, 2000, and I have promised to show Dana Gardner a signature bird of Beaver Creek, an Acadian flycatcher. We cross the swinging footbridge to where the valley narrows, the forest increases in density, and wood nettles cover the forest floor. Soon the sharp explosive *peet-suh* song of the flycatcher reaches our ears. We follow the sound until we see the olive-gray bird perching on a low branch, flicking its tail and singing. We note its eye ring, yellow lower mandible, and white wingbars. Suddenly, it flies from its perch to capture an insect in midair, a foraging technique that is common to all flycatchers.

The Acadian is one of eleven *Empidonax*, or king of the gnats, flycatchers that breed in North America. These very small birds look so much alike that the only way to identify them safely is by their songs. Habitat, however, offers a helpful clue. The Acadian breeds in mature deciduous forests, in swampy areas, or near streams across the eastern states except for the far north. Southeast Minnesota is the northern edge of its breeding range. Wintering grounds are in mature tropical forests of Central America and northern South America.

In courtship mates engage in erratic, rapid chases and the male hovers above the perched female. Long-term pair bonds and strong fidelity to breeding territory are characteristics of these birds. For a nest, the female builds a loose basket of plant fibers that she weaves together with spider and caterpillar silk and suspends within the horizontal fork of a branch well out from the main trunk of a tree four to fifty feet above ground. She usually lays three eggs and incubates them for two weeks. Both parents feed their babies until they fledge about two weeks after hatching and for around twelve days after they leave the nest. If the female begins a second clutch, her mate feeds the first brood alone.

In Minnesota and elsewhere, the Acadian flycatcher is a species of conservation concern. Because the bird is nowhere abundant, it is particularly vulnerable to habitat loss on both its wintering and its breeding grounds. Due to fragmentation of North American forests, this species must nest close to woodland edges, which commonly results in brood parasitism by the edge-loving brown-headed cowbird. However, populations appear stable at present except in Florida and the southern Appalachians, where significant declines have occurred.

Beaver Creek continues to be a reliable area for Acadian flycatchers. Shattuck Creek, which has similar habitat and is only a few miles from my home, is another place where every spring and early summer I can count on hearing the *peet-suh* song.

Northern Shrike

Lanius excubitor

My husband and I began watching birds at about the same time as did our neighbors, Erik and Kathy Erickson. Our first winter, we occasionally noticed a sudden disappearance of our feeder birds, which we soon connected to the presence of a northern shrike, a species that fascinated all four of us because, although a songbird itself, it is a fierce predator of other birds, including those that equal it in size, such as mockingbirds. With fascination and dread, we would watch the black-masked shrike, perched near the top of a small tree, waiting for the slight movement of some hapless goldfinch or cardinal.

We were torn between wanting this beautiful species to capture a meal and feeling sorry for the poor birds, voles, or other rodents it would kill by pounding its bill into their skulls and using the hook on its bill to sever their spinal cords. We knew about but had not yet witnessed the shrike's habit of storing prey, which also includes large insects, by impaling them on a thorn or fence barb, thus earning it the name butcher bird.

To attract a mate, a male shrike may build up a cache, which he defends by singing a complex song that includes imitations of other birds. Bonding displays involve head bowing, wing and tail spreading, and mate feeding. Nests are in open spruce woods or alder and willow scrub on the edge of the tundra. In a small tree or large shrub, both sexes build a bulky nest of twigs and bark strips lined with feathers. Incubation of the four to seven eggs is mostly by the female and lasts about sixteen days. Both parents feed the nestlings until they fledge about three weeks after hatching and for several weeks thereafter.

In fall, these birds migrate into southern Canada and the northern United States. During years when vole populations plummet, they will move south in an irruptive manner similar to northern owls. Upper Midwest birders usually assume that a shrike in winter is a northern and one in summer is a loggerhead, the only other North American member of this genus, a more southern bird whose behavior and appearance are similar to its relative's. The loggerhead has recently declined in population, possibly due to the effects of pesticides and changes in habitat, factors that may also affect the northern species.

In recent years, I have seen few northern shrikes in my yard, but almost every winter I find one or two of them at the top of a small tree or shrub in an open area. Last winter, while birding in Fillmore County with my friends Fred and Carol, I saw something I had never witnessed before—a shrike feeding on a small rodent it had impaled on a thorn.

Philadelphia Vireo

Vireo philadelphicus

On a 1987 field trip, my first birding mentor, Anne Marie Plunkett, introduced me to vireos, the small foliage-gleaning songbirds that look like some wood warblers except for their larger heads and thicker bills. On that trip, we saw red-eyed, yellow-throated, and blue-headed vireos. When I returned home, I found all three species, which I could probably have found earlier if I had thought to look for them. I soon added the warbling vireo to my yard list, but it wasn't until 1993 that I saw a Philadelphia, the least common of the five species likely to occur in my area.

Anne Marie also introduced me to the century-old Fillmore County diaries of Johan Hvoslef, where I found numerous references to correspondence with Thomas S. Roberts, who made extensive use of Hvoslef's records in *The Birds of Minnesota*. Regarding the Philadelphia vireo, Roberts wrote that it was an uncommon migrant throughout the state and that Hvoslef was the only observer who had reported the bird in considerable numbers.

Breeding occurs primarily in second-growth forests of poplars, willows, and alders across much of Canada, where the male sings to defend his territory and, as part of the breeding ritual, fluffs his feathers, fans his tail, and sways from side to side while he and the female rapidly vibrate their wings. Both sexes build the nest, a pendulous cup of grasses, bark strips, spider webs, and cocoons hanging ten to ninety feet above ground from a horizontal forked twig in a deciduous tree. Both parents incubate the four eggs for about two weeks and feed the nestlings mostly insects that they catch in midair or secure by hovering above foliage or hanging upside down from small branches. Young birds fledge about two weeks after hatching.

In the Upper Midwest, we see Philadelphias most commonly during September, when they are en route to their wintering grounds in the relatively dry lowland and foothill forests of Central America. In 2005, they were more common than usual and, for the first time, I observed one singing. Unlike most songbirds, vireos will sing all day long from spring through autumn and males often sing while incubating. Because the Philadelphia's song of short phrases is similar to that of the red-eyed vireo and its appearance is similar to the warbling vireo and Tennessee warbler, one must pay close attention in order to identify this species correctly.

On its exceptionally long migration routes, the Philadelphia faces many dangers, not the least of which is flying around the Gulf of Mexico in fall and, pushed by southerly winds, directly across it in spring. Despite Hvoslef's considerable numbers, the density of this species remains low, which makes it especially vulnerable to losses in migration. Habitat degradation, particularly in Central America, is also worrisome.

Brown Creeper

Certhia americana

In early spring, on a dark, rainy day, I hear a high, thin *see* so quiet it could be my imagination or a ringing in my ears. On the chance that it's a bird, I look on ends of branches for a black-capped chickadee, high in trees for a golden-crowned kinglet, and along trunks of trees for a brown creeper. Of the three species, only the creeper emits a single syllable, but counting these wispy call notes in the field is difficult, especially when louder forest sounds mix with them. To my delight, I find a creeper using its long, stiffened woodpeckerlike tail for support and its long, curved claws to crawl up and around the trunk of a large elm in search of an insect to remove from a crevice in the bark with its thin, decurved, tweezerlike bill. Soon the little bird flies down to the base of another tree and begins its long journey spiraling up again. Insects are this species' main source of food, but it also eats some seeds and nuts.

Brown creepers are members of the Certhiidae family, which consists of seven species worldwide. All are similar in appearance and behavior. Six species inhabit Europe and Asia. Only the brown occurs in North America. I see this small, nondescript bird most often during spring and fall migration, but Johan Hvoslef often reported creepers in his Lanesboro yard in winter and they frequently appear during Christmas Bird Counts throughout the Upper Midwest. Breeding takes place in southern Canada and our western and northeastern states where some birds are permanent residents. Others migrate to the southeastern states and Central America for the winter.

Creepers may seem more uncommon than they are not only because their quiet calls and equally quiet, more complex songs make them difficult to locate, but because their pattern of brown, buff, black, and white feathers looks like bark. This intimacy with bark and the trunks of large deciduous or coniferous trees also extends to breeding behavior. In courtship the male performs twisting flights and rapidly spirals around trunks in pursuit of the female. The female, with some help from her mate, builds a half-cup nest of bark, twigs, moss, and spider silk that fits behind a strip of bark still attached to a tree. Her mate may feed her on the nest while she sits on her five to six eggs for about two weeks. Both parents feed the nestlings, which fledge when they are thirteen to sixteen days old.

Although brown creeper populations are currently healthy throughout most of their range, some populations have declined due to the cutting of mature forests. I am grateful that I live in a mature forest where I can find these small, cryptically plumaged birds quietly inching up trees in search of food.

Winter Wren

Troglodytes troglodytes

In early April I hear a welcome *hiccup* call, surprisingly loud for such a small bird. I see movement on a fallen log near our spring. With each *hiccup*, the winter wren, its tail raised to the maximum extent, bobs up and down on its tiny toes, tempting me to anthropomorphize and assign it a sweet, exuberant, and cocky personality. I don't know when or if I would have noticed the simultaneous calling and bobbing behavior if Carol Schumacher, who has meticulously observed this species, hadn't told me about it.

Of the five wren species that we are likely to see in the Upper Midwest, the winter wren, with heavy barring on its belly, flanks, and tail, is our smallest and darkest. It most closely resembles the house wren, which is larger and has less barring. By the time the larger bird appears in my woods, its cousin has usually left for breeding grounds in the coniferous forests of Canada and just inside our northern border from Minnesota to the East Coast.

Although relatively common, the winter wren is difficult to see because it dwells in dense vegetation close to the ground, where it forages for insects among foliage, twigs, and rocks. However, during breeding season the male flies to a high perch from which he sings to defend his territory and attract a mate. His song, among the prettiest in the avian world, is a complicated series of high, tinkling trills and tumbling warbles. In display, he squats, quivers his wings, and moves his tail from side to side while singing or calling. In any kind of natural cavity, including holes among roots, in rotting stumps, and in streambanks or crevices among rocks, the male, like other wrens, may build several dummy nests. When the female picks a site, both sexes build a cup nest of grass, moss, rootlets, feathers, and animal hair. The female lays five or six eggs that she incubates for about two weeks. Both parents feed the babies. The male, who often has more than one mate, may be feeding more than one set of offspring at the same time. Young birds leave the nest about nineteen days after hatching.

During the last half of September, I begin listening again for the *hiccup* call and looking for winter wrens fussing among the roots and rocks near our spring. The latest I have seen these birds is November 18, but others, including Johan Hvoslef, have seen them near perennial streams in the depths of Minnesota winters. Many spend the winter as far north as Iowa and all stay within the United States. Fortunately, we may enjoy this species for years to come because populations appear to be increasing partly due to plentiful habitat and the bird's ability to nest in a wide variety of small cavities.

Townsend's Solitaire

Myadestes townsendi

On January 18, 2004, John Hockema found a Townsend's solitaire in a red cedar, a common species of juniper, about ten miles from my home. Although I had looked for solitaires before, I had never found one. I hoped my luck was about to change, but my search that day was unsuccessful. The next day Craig Mandel led a field trip to Fillmore County for his Twin Cities–area Audubon Club. I met them at the solitaire place, but in spite of looking carefully and playing a recording of the bird's clear, single-note call, we were unable to find this thrush from the western states and western Canada that sometimes winters as far east as the Upper Midwest, where it maintains a solitary territory in the middle of a supply of cedar berries. Some compensation for our lack of success came with the sightings of a northern shrike and overwintering flickers and robins on the way to my woods, where the group found further compensation in watching a tufted titmouse at our feeders, a species that is uncommon elsewhere in Minnesota.

During breeding season, the solitaire's diet expands to include worms, spiders, and insects that it finds in coniferous mountain forests. It hunts by hovering to pick insects and berries from foliage, pouncing on prey that it finds on the ground, and flying out from a perch to catch prey in the air. Although the bird is similar to flycatchers in its slender shape, long tail, and method of catching insects, the complex, warbling song that the male sings to defend his territory proves his membership in the thrush family.

Solitaires use pine needles, bark strips, twigs, and grass to construct a shallow cup nest in a dirt bank, in the crevice of a cliff, under tree roots, or under another overhanging shelter. Ornithologists know that the clutch size is usually three to five, that the incubation period is about eleven days, and that both parents feed their babies, which have spotted breasts like other young thrushes, but they know little else of this bird's breeding biology. In his 1926 book *Birds of Western Canada*, P. A. Taverner wrote, "A bird typical of the high mountain solitudes, well named Solitaire. Its unobtrusive dull grey colour, glorious song, and romantic habitat and name, surround it with an air of mystery that piques the imagination."

I suspect that solitaires have occasionally wintered among our cedar trees in years when they have wandered east due to poor supplies of berries in their usual western range. My inability to find one may be due to lack of luck or diligence, so I will continue to look for this bird, which my friends say is not so difficult to find, especially since the species is doing well and faces few significant threats.

Veery

Catharus fuscescens

Grass was still wet with morning dew. Beaver Creek tumbled over rocks at our feet. Sun reached between the leaves of deciduous trees to touch false rue anemones, jack-in-the-pulpits, wild ginger, and wood nettles in the dense understory. My husband and I sat on a bench along our favorite trail in Beaver Creek Valley State Park about thirty-five miles from our home. An Acadian flycatcher sang its *peet-suh* song and a Louisiana waterthrush sang *see-you, see-you, see-you, chew, chew, to-wee*. We had earlier seen the elusive cerulean warbler and heard its high, musical trill. As we sat on the bench, an ethereal song reached our ears, enhancing our romantic mood. It was a rolling series of descending, breezy notes with harmonics reminiscent of a violin, something like *vee-ur, vee-ur, vee-ur*. Soon we heard another veery answering the first. This concert by probable mates continued for several minutes, but we never saw the little thrushes.

Veeries are difficult to see because their brown upperparts and white breasts with brown spots look like their surroundings as they move about in low vegetation foraging for berries or on the forest floor searching for insects by turning over leaves with their bills. These thrushes are similar in behavior and appearance to the gray-cheeked, Swainson's, and hermit thrushes. All occur in our region during migration but only the veery, which breeds in moist, deciduous forests of western Canada and most of our northern states, is a summer resident as far south as southern Minnesota, Wisconsin, and Ohio.

Migrating north from his winter home east of the Andes, the male veery arrives on breeding grounds before the female and sings to defend his territory. In courtship, he chases the female and sings duets with her. The female places her cup nest of weeds, twigs, and bark fibers with a base of dry leaves on or just above the ground. She incubates her five or six eggs for about two weeks. Both parents feed their young for about eleven days in the nest and for three or four weeks after they begin to hop around in the surrounding vegetation.

Due to the fragmentation of northern forests, nests of this species frequently fall victim to the brown-headed cowbird. The veery also faces dangers because of its long migration; the loss of habitat and food at either end of its route and at stopovers along the way often leads to its demise. According to the North American Breeding Bird Survey, populations have declined thirty percent since 1966 when the survey began.

I have never observed a veery in my woods, perhaps because the understory is neither sufficiently damp nor dense. But I usually have to travel only five miles to Shattuck Creek, much of which the state has preserved as a natural area, to hear this little thrush sing its ethereal song.

Wood Thrush

Hylocichla mustelina

The simplest description of a wood thrush song is a flutelike *eee-o-lay*, but that does not describe its complexity. One summer evening at twilight, I sat on my porch, watching mist rise from trees and grass. The rain had just passed. When the song began, I closed my eyes and listened to the rising then falling notes, music rolling around the clearing, bouncing off the edge of the forest as the thrush harmonized with himself.

All bird vocalizations come from the syrinx, a unique avian organ located in most birds at the junction of the trachea and the two primary bronchi. Muscles attached to the syrinx control the quality of sound by modifying vibrations of membranes when air pushes past them from the lungs. Birds with the most highly evolved syringes are able to sing through both bronchi simultaneously, allowing for harmonics and the production of two notes at once.

When the male wood thrush arrives on his breeding grounds somewhere in the moist, deciduous forests from the East Coast to the eastern Great Plains, he sings to establish and defend his territory. His aggression toward other males involves body postures, chases, and singing duels. When the female arrives, singing becomes part of courtship along with rapid, circular chases close to the ground. In the vertical fork of a tree or on a horizontal branch ten to fifteen feet high, the female builds a cup nest of grass, leaves, moss, bark, and bits of paper with a middle layer of mud and a lining of rootlets. She incubates her three or four eggs for about two weeks. Both parents feed the nestlings insects and berries that they find on the ground or in shrubs. Fledging occurs at about twelve days of age, after which each parent feeds half the brood. If the female begins a second brood, the male feeds all the fledglings alone.

In fall, wood thrushes migrate at night in mixed-species flocks south across the Gulf of Mexico to their wintering grounds in the tropical forests of Mexico and Central America. Like other nocturnal migrants, they fly at low altitudes, which often leads to collisions with towers and buildings. Collisions are not the only dangers these thrushes face. Increasingly, fragmentation of forests, especially in the Midwest, results in nest predation by crows, grackles, and blue jays along with parasitism by cowbirds, all of which benefit from edge habitats. Habitat destruction on tropical wintering grounds is also a concern. Since 1966, populations of this species have declined forty-three percent.

Because their rusty upperparts and white underparts with black spots blend with vegetation in the forest understory where they forage, I rarely see wood thrushes, but their eloquent dawn and dusk songs, which I hope will continue to grace my woods, more than make up for their lack of visibility.

Brown Thrasher

Toxostoma rufum

For a moment I thought the brown-backed bird with dark spots on its white breast foraging among the gooseberry bushes was a wood thrush. Then I saw its long, slightly decurved bill and long tail and knew it was a brown thrasher. On looking closer, I noticed that its breast had fine, brown streaks instead of spots. Another clue was the bird's presence in shrubbery rather than in the forest understory, where wood thrushes dwell. The next morning I heard rich, melodic phrases coming from the top of a white oak near our workshop. The thrasher sang each phrase twice, which differentiated its song from the single phrases of the gray catbird and triple phrases of the northern mockingbird. Thrashers, catbirds, and mockingbirds belong to the New World family Mimidae. All mimids have complex songs and often weave the songs of other species into their repertoires. Although the brown thrasher mimics less than its relatives, it has one of the largest song repertoires of all North American birds.

This species breeds in dense brush around the edges of woods, swamps, or suburban neighborhoods from the East Coast west into the Great Plains. The male sings to defend his territory. In courtship he sings softly while approaching a female. Either bird may then pick up a stick or leaf and present it to the other. Working together, the male and female gather twigs, grass, leaves, and rootlets to build a bulky, loosely constructed nest on or close to the ground. Both parents incubate their four eggs for about two weeks. During this time, when danger approaches, they rely on the camouflage their plumage provides and do not flush until the last minute. Both the mother and father feed their nestlings berries, nuts, and insects that they find by foraging in shrubs and trees or by using their long, strong bills to dig in the soil or "thrash" the ground. The young birds leave the nest at nine to thirteen days of age, after which the mother will likely begin a second brood while the father cares for the first. If enough time remains before fall migration or the onset of winter, the adults may attempt a third brood.

All brown thrashers winter within the United States. Southern birds are usually permanent residents. Northern birds leave for the Gulf states in September or October. When they return to the Upper Midwest in April, I usually see or hear one in my yard, but it doesn't stay long before moving to a more open brushy place to breed. I don't see as many of these birds as I once did. Populations are slowly declining throughout their range due to loss of habitat with the regrowth of forests in the East and Upper Midwest and the elimination of fencerows in the Great Plains.

Bohemian Waxwing

Bombycilla garrulus

Whenever I see cedar waxwings I marvel at their intricate, colorful markings—warm, brown bodies and crests, black masks, yellowish bellies, a spot of bright red on their wings, and yellow-tipped tails. I watch how flocks in flight turn in unison and how individuals fly out to catch insects in midair. I relish the sight of fifty inebriated birds whistling and flying erratically as they consume vast numbers of fermented red cedar berries.

Taking the advice of other birders, I always look carefully at these birds in hopes of seeing Bohemian waxwings among them. Both species are nomadic, but in winter Bohemians normally inhabit wooded, semi-open, berry-rich country from western Canada and the western states to northern Minnesota and only rarely, when food is scarce, wander into my area. Because of their similar habits and markings, I feared I wouldn't be able to distinguish Bohemians from cedars. Then on December 29, 2000, I saw seven large waxwings with grayish bellies and rufous undertail coverts in our crabapple tree. I knew immediately that they were Bohemians, whose name comes from their seemingly care-free and wandering life-style. The birds stayed through December 31, by which time they had eaten all the crabapples.

In summer this species lives and breeds in the boreal forests and muskegs of western Canada and Alaska. Nesting, which is later than for most passerines, takes place from June through August with the midsummer ripening of juniper berries and other fruit. In courtship mates perch together, fluff their feathers, and pass a berry back and forth. Both sexes gather twigs, grass, rootlets, spider webs, and moss, often from old nests, to build a cup-shaped nest on the horizontal branch of a tree, often a spruce. Although the female incubates their four to six eggs alone for about two weeks, the male helps feed the nestlings, which fledge around fourteen to eighteen days after hatching. Young birds join their parents' flock and may remain with it through their first fall and winter.

When I spotted the Bohemians in my crabapple tree, I reported the sighting to Dana Gardner, who was visiting in Lanesboro before traveling to northern Minnesota to witness the 2000–01 irruption of northern owls. Although he had never seen this species, he declined my invitation, saying the birds would surely make an appearance in the North Country. Unfortunately he didn't find the birds either that winter or on his trip to witness the record-breaking owl irruption of 2004–05. Fortunately, he may yet have the opportunity to observe the wandering Bohemians, as populations have been increasing since the late 1970s due to regrowth of habitats containing fruiting shrubs on former agricultural lands and the elimination of the pesticide DDT, to which the birds were susceptible because of their tendency to feed on insect outbreaks.

Blue-winged Warbler

Vermivora pinus

My heart beats faster when in early May I hear *beee-BZZZZ* coming from the brushy area along my driveway. Did my old ears actually hear the high-pitched, buzzy song, or did I imagine it because I was anxiously awaiting the return of the blue-winged warbler from its winter home in the evergreen and semideciduous forests of Mexico and Central America? I look up at our power line, a favorite perch of this stunning bird, and there it is— blue-gray wings, black eyeline, bright yellow underparts—vigorously singing.

Blue-wings and about thirty-five other wood warblers, all small, active insectivores, migrate through or breed in our region each year. During the late 1800s, blue-wings began moving north from Tennessee and Kentucky. Southeast Minnesota is now the northwestern edge of their breeding range, so I am able to observe them from spring through autumn, along with watching the pleasure they give my guests, who have few opportunities to view these buzzy beauties.

One day last spring, I watched two males chasing each other while singing variations of their song. A lone female perched nearby. I knew that, after choosing a mate, she would use dead leaves, grass, and plant fibers to build a narrow, deep, inverted cone on the ground or attached to surrounding weed stems. She would incubate her five eggs alone for ten days, then both she and her mate would find insects and spiders for their young by probing with their bills into curled leaves, buds, and flowers of shrubs and trees. I once saw two downy babies, which meant they were less than two weeks old, perched in a small bush, but I have never found a nest.

As the blue-wing moves north it is gradually replacing its close relative, the golden-winged warbler, who in response is extending its own range northward. Where territories overlap, these species often interbreed, resulting in the Brewster's warbler, a hybrid that has a yellow head, yellow throat, and white belly, or the Lawrence's warbler, a rare second-generation hybrid that has a yellow crown, yellow belly, black throat, and black cheeks.

Before May 14, 1988, I had seen neither hybrid. On that day, when Alden Risser was leading the Fillmore County Birders along Shattuck Creek, his favorite birdwatching area, Chris Hockema, our youngest member, located a singing blue-winged warbler that looked different. Although he had never seen one before, Doc Risser knew immediately that the bird was a Lawrence's warbler. He said the sighting was one of the best birthday presents he had ever received. Until then we hadn't known it was his birthday. Our experience that day was particularly poignant because we knew our chances of finding any of these little relatives were decreasing due to habitat loss from human development in the North and deforestation in tropical America.

Northern Parula

Parula americana

On July 5, 2004, while exploring the bluffs above the Root River near Lanesboro, Dana Gardner and I walked through a restored prairie and a narrow strip of hardwoods mixed with large white pines to an overlook, where we gazed across a valley that showed no signs of human habitation. We sat there silently, listening to the songs of birds and the river. When we finally broke our silence and walked back through the trees, we heard a rising, buzzy trill that ended abruptly with a lower note. At first, neither of us could place the song, perhaps because it is not common in our area. After hearing several more trills, however, I suddenly realized that the songster was a northern parula warbler. We walked back and forth searching the treetops where this species spends much of its time flying out to catch insects in the air or finding them while hopping among leaves, hovering over foliage, or hanging upside down on twigs. The name parula, meaning a diminutive *Parus*, the genus name for chickadees, comes from the warbler's acrobatic chickadeelike foraging methods. Sadly, despite our scrutiny of the treetops, we were unable to find the tiny bird with blue-gray upperparts, white belly, and blue and rufous bands across its yellow throat and breast.

The parula's presence in midsummer surprised us because it usually occurs in our region only during migration and then only infrequently. This warbler is primarily an eastern bird, breeding west to northern Minnesota and down through eastern Texas, excluding a wide swath south of the Great Lakes to Arkansas that lacks its preferred nesting materials. Pairs often return to the same breeding site in successive years. The male sings while accompanying his mate on trips to and from the nest, which is a small pouch of twigs and Spanish moss or hanging tree lichens called usnea. In the absence of such supplies, dangling clumps of pine needles or rubbish left by floods in branches may suffice. Dana and I wondered if the bird we heard had a mate who had used the alternate materials, but we knew such a nest would be nearly impossible to find.

After constructing the nest, the female lays four or five eggs and, with help from the male, incubates them for twelve to fourteen days. Both parents feed their young, which fledge about ten days after hatching. Their time to independence remains a mystery, but by fall they are ready to fly to wintering grounds in the semi-evergreen forests of Florida, Mexico, Central America, or the West Indies.

Because of the parula's dependence on mature forests with hanging moss or lichens for breeding, it is of moderate conservation concern. Currently, however, the overall population appears stable, with declines in the Mississippi River Valley and southern coastal plains and increases in the North and the Appalachians.

Cerulean Warbler

Dendroica cerulea

Our June 1989 Fillmore County Birders field trip to Forestville State Park in southeastern Minnesota was nearly over but the best was yet to come. While lingering in the parking lot and scanning the trees with our binoculars, we discovered a cerulean warbler, aptly named for its sky-blue head and back. Difficult to locate because of its small size, constant activity, and habit of foraging for insects in the tops of tall deciduous trees, the cerulean is usually first identified by its song, a rising three-part musical buzz. The sighting of what was a life bird for most of us was a perfect way to end our day.

Ceruleans are hard to find for another reason. According to the North American Breeding Bird Survey, populations have declined between four and five percent per year over the last four decades, one of the steepest declines of any warbler species. Habitat loss and degradation are to blame. Breeding takes place exclusively in mature hardwood forests with high canopies in the northeast and east central states, formerly with the greatest abundance in the old-growth forests of the Ohio and Mississippi River valleys. With the spread of human development, the large tracts of woodlands that are required for breeding, foraging, and avoiding cowbirds have largely disappeared.

Because of the difficulty observing the cerulean, our knowledge of its breeding biology is incomplete. The female likely constructs the shallow nest of grass, plant stems, bark, moss, and lichen, which she binds with spider silk to a high horizontal branch far from the trunk of a hardwood tree. She incubates her three or four eggs for about twelve days. Both parents feed their young. Fledging likely occurs about ten days after hatching.

In early fall ceruleans begin their journeys to the canopies of subtropical forests on the eastern slopes of the Andes mountains from Colombia to Venezuela, Ecuador, and Peru, a winter habitat that is rapidly being replaced by plantings of coffee beans and coca to serve a rising demand for coffee and cocaine-based drugs.

Fortunately, efforts are under way to preserve habitat. In 2005 the American Bird Conservancy and the Colombian conservation group Fundación ProAves announced the creation of a five-hundred–acre preserve of subtropical forest in Colombia to protect the cerulean warbler. U.S. national wildlife refuges also provide essential habitat and Audubon's Important Bird Areas program supports the conservation of habitat vital to this warbler and other species.

Although ceruleans are becoming ever harder to find, July 2005 reports from Iowa birder Shane Patterson were encouraging. While birding in eastern Iowa, he saw these elusive warblers in Effigy Mounds National Monument, White Pine Hollow Preserve, Backbone State Park, Yellow River State Forest, and five other areas.

Prothonotary Warbler

Protonotaria citrea

A series of single-syllable, ringing *zweet* notes tells my husband and me that we have come to the right place, a bottomland pool of the Mississippi River in southeastern Minnesota. Looking up at overhanging branches in the direction of the sound, we find a golden-headed bird with golden sides and underparts, a prothonotary warbler, whose name refers to the bright yellow hood of a scribe in the Catholic church.

Carol Schumacher has extensively studied the prothonotary's appearance, vocalizations, and breeding biology. Most years she finds it nesting in a small tree cavity on Prairie Island near her Winona home. As she has done with many species, Carol has told me so much about this warbler that I am no longer able to distinguish what I have learned from her, from books, or from my own observations.

The prothonotary breeds in wooded swamps, flooded bottomland forests, and along slow-moving rivers mostly in the Southeast, but over the years it has also moved north to breed, especially along the Mississippi River Valley. The male arrives on the nesting grounds about a week before the female and establishes a territory by singing and intimidating intruding males with visual displays and chases. He may build dummy nests by placing moss into a natural cavity, an abandoned woodpecker hole, or an artificial nest box low over standing water. When a potential mate arrives, he flutters his wings and spreads his tail feathers. The female invites copulation by quivering her wings and elevating her tail. She builds a complete nest by filling a cavity with moss, leaves, twigs, bark, and rootlets. She lays four to six eggs and incubates them for about two weeks.

Both parents glean snails and insects for their nestlings from leaves and branches close to the ground. They also catch insects in midair and probe for food in bark while crawling along trunks. Young birds fledge about ten days after hatching, at which time they can supposedly swim should they land in the water. Each parent feeds half the fledglings unless the mother nests again, in which case the father becomes the sole caregiver.

In spite of help it has received from the placement of nest boxes, the prothonotary has declined by thirty percent over the last forty years, due in part to the clearing and fragmenting of bottomland forests on its breeding range, which exacerbates cowbird parasitism and results in drying of the seasonally flooded woods that the warbler requires. Destruction of tropical lowland forests on its Central and South American winter range also presents difficulties.

Fortunately, plans to restore wooded wetlands in the Mississippi River Valley should result in increased nesting opportunities for this warbler and increased opportunities for birders to hear its ringing *zweet* notes.

Louisiana Waterthrush

Seiurus motacilla

Whenever I see a clear-flowing forest stream with exposed rocks or mossy islands and tree roots digging into vertical dirt banks, I think of the Louisiana waterthrush, a thrush-like warbler that bobs up and down as it walks at the water's edge, picking directly at insects and crustaceans or turning over leaves to find them. The bobbing motion is useful in identification but not sufficient, because the closely related northern waterthrush, which has the same brown upperparts, similarly streaked underparts, and similar whitish eyebrow stripes, bobs in the same manner. I usually need to hear the clear, slurred whistles and jumbled descending chirps of the Louisiana to distinguish it from its relative. Another clue is time of year; in summer the northern waterthrush is not present in my area.

Since the mid 1800s the Louisiana, which once bred only in the southeastern states, has been gradually extending its range, especially along the Mississippi River and its tributaries. The northern edge of its territory now crosses from lower New England to southeast Minnesota. According to Thomas S. Roberts in *The Birds of Minnesota*, the first report of this warbler in the state came from Johan Hvoslef in 1883, who found it in the Root River Valley near Lanesboro.

The male waterthrush defends a long, narrow breeding territory along a stream by engaging in vigorous chases and countersinging with neighboring males. Chases also occur between potential mates. With some help from the male in gathering material, the female builds a cup nest of leaves, moss, twigs, bark, rootlets, and ferns, which she conceals in a crevice or among tree roots along a streambank. Hatching of the three to six eggs takes place after about two weeks of incubation by the mother. Both parents feed the babies, which leave the nest when they are around ten days old. By August, young birds and adults are on their way to wintering grounds along clear forest streams in the lowland woods of Mexico, Central America, and northern South America.

This species is of high conservation importance because of its low overall density, frequent victimization by cowbirds, and dependence on healthy forest streams, which are also of conservation concern due to erosion and contamination from agricultural runoff.

In Minnesota, one reliable place to find the Louisiana is Beaver Creek Valley State Park. In 2005, Rochester birder Bill Bruins, who surveyed the park for six years, saw six waterthrushes there in one day and found one nest. Every spring I find at least one of these uncommon warblers along Shattuck Creek, but I have never found a nest. Healthy forest streams in Iowa also attract this bird. In July 2005 Shane Patterson observed Louisianas at seven sites in the northeastern part of the state, including Yellow River State Forest, where he saw parents feeding two fledglings.

Hooded Warbler

Wilsonia citrina

On June 2, 1989, I stopped to rest on a bench in my woods near a dry ravine, where I nearly fell asleep. I must have been hearing a particular song for awhile before I consciously realized I was hearing something different—loud, clear, slurred notes sounding like *dee-da, dee-da, dee-DEE-oh*, with the penultimate syllable higher and louder than the others. The songster had bright yellow underparts and a black hood enclosing a yellow face and forehead. I hurried home to call Anne Marie Plunkett, who agreed with my identification of the first hooded warbler ever reported in Fillmore County. The same day, I spoke with University of Minnesota ornithologist Bruce Fall, who has a special interest in this species. He told me that the warbler's normal range is in large tracts of mature, uninterrupted deciduous forest with dense shrub layers in the southeastern states, but that it regularly wanders into Minnesota. He said since the breeding season had already begun, I should look for a nest.

The male hooded returns to the same breeding area as in previous years, where he sings to defend his territory and engages in chases with intruding males. The female usually has a different territory and mate each year. In courtship, both sexes fan their tails, revealing large white spots on their outer tail feathers. The female chooses a site low to the ground along a stream or dry ravine and uses spider silk to weave a cup nest of soft inner bark, fine grasses, and plant down with an outer layer of dead leaves and leaf skeletons that provides camouflage. She lays four eggs and incubates them for about twelve days. Both parents feed the babies until they leave the nest at nine days of age, after which each adult cares for half the brood for up to five weeks, during which time the mother and her dependents leave the territory. The parents glean insects for their young and themselves from leaf surfaces in shrubs or make short flights to catch flying prey.

Because of their dependency on habitats that are rapidly disappearing—large, mature, deciduous forests on their breeding grounds and lowland tropical forests in eastern Mexico and Central America where they winter, hooded warblers are of moderate conservation concern.

Although Minnesota is not part of this warbler's usual range, Bruce Fall and others have monitored as many as thirty-five males returning to breeding territory in the Murphy-Hanrehan Park Preserve in the Minneapolis area, where the number of nests parasitized by the cowbird generally equals those that successfully fledge young. Sporadic reports come from elsewhere in Minnesota every year, but in spite of carefully looking and listening each May and June, I have never again found a hooded warbler in the ravine where one sang in 1989.

Yellow-breasted Chat

Icteria virens

Every day for a week in June 2000, I heard a whistling sound coming from a brushy hillside a mile from my house. The sound tapped into a vague memory that I could not place. Then one day, while listening to a recording of warbler vocalizations, as I do now and then to refresh my memory, I heard the whistle of a yellow-breasted chat and thought it could be my mystery bird. During breeding season the chat is common across most of the country but is uncommon to rare in Minnesota, Wisconsin, and parts of North and South Dakota, where a sighting creates excitement in the birding community.

This species' large size, thick tanagerlike bill, its habit of flying with floppy wingbeats and dangling legs, and its odd vocalizations reminiscent of a catbird make it the most atypical warbler. Where other warblers are difficult to locate because of their constant activity and small sizes, the chat is rarely seen because it is a solitary species that usually remains hidden in dense, low scrub where it forages for insects and berries. In *Birds of Western Canada*, P. A. Taverner says the chat "is the spirit of the tangled thickets and brushy wastes and like a spirit it comes and goes unseen, but not unheard. It laughs and cackles, whistles, and mocks."

In courtship, the male points his bill up and sways from side to side. He flies up singing, hovers, and then drops slowly with legs dangling back to his perch. In dense shrubs or tangled vines, his mate constructs an outer layer of leaves and straw that provides support for an inner nest of vine bark and fine weed stems. She sits on her three or four eggs for about eleven days. Both adults feed their young, which leave the nest about eight days after hatching. Although chats often play host to cowbird babies, and nest predation by raccoons and other animals is common, current populations are apparently stable.

With the help of Minnesota birder Phil Chu, who came to my woods to see the resident tufted titmice, I was finally able to identify the bird I heard in June 2000. I told Phil about the possible chat and, after observing the titmice, he accompanied me to the brushy hill where he played a recording to draw the bird into sight. Before long, we heard not only the whistles but a full repertoire of squeaks and rattles. Soon the chat appeared and stayed where we could see it for about half an hour. From then until July 6, more than twenty people observed the bird, which was apparently a lone male. Every year since then I have waited for the big warbler to return to the same area from his wintering grounds in Mexico or Central America but have always been disappointed.

Summer Tanager

Piranga rubra

A greenish yellow bird with blotchy redness around the head and chest flew out from behind our woodshed. My first thought that it was a scarlet tanager in fall molt couldn't be right because the date was May 7. After a quick look in a field guide, I identified the bird as a male summer tanager in his first breeding plumage. Fully adult males are all red and adult females come in shades of yellow, green, and gray.

Unlike the bright red, black-winged scarlet tanager that graces deciduous forests of the Upper Midwest during breeding season, the summer tanager breeds mostly in dry, open woods of the southeastern states as far north as south central Iowa. It is an infrequent migrant in Minnesota. Thomas S. Roberts reported only two records before 1932. Since then, sporadic reports have continued along with several discoveries of hybridization with scarlet tanagers. In 2003 near the Twin Cities, James Mattsson and ornithologist Bruce Fall each found a male summer tanager that had paired with a female scarlet tanager. Both pairs raised a brown-headed cowbird.

Four species of tanagers regularly breed in North America, but about two hundred brightly colored species varying from red to blue, green, and purple occur in Central and South America. In his 1989 book *Life of the Tanager*, Alexander Skutch tells the stories of these birds. In spring the male summer tanager, like many of his relatives, sings to defend breeding territory, courts a female by chasing her, and eventually accompanies his mate on nest-building trips. The nest, usually placed on a high horizontal branch of an oak or cottonwood tree, is a loose cup of grass, bark, leaves, and spider webs. The female incubates her three to five eggs for about twelve days and both parents feed their young, whose age of fledging is unknown.

This species not only builds its nest in the treetops but also spends most of its time there foraging for insects. Wasp larvae, wasps, and bees are its specialties, earning it the nickname beebird and the title of pest around apiaries. Before eating a bee or wasp that it catches in flight, the tanager takes it to a perch, beats it against a branch, and wipes it on the branch to remove the stinger. Berries and fruit also provide food, especially on wintering grounds in lowland forests and scrublands from central Mexico to Brazil.

Populations have not changed much in recent years except for declines in a few localities. Primary dangers include habitat loss and collisions with towers and tall buildings during night migration. The bird in my yard on May 7, 1999, soon flew out of sight and I never saw it again, but since then I have looked more carefully at every red or partly red bird I see.

Lark Sparrow

Chondestes grammacus

Unlike many sparrows, the lark sparrow is easy to identify because of its chestnut head pattern, black breast spot, white outer tail feathers, large size, and varied song of liquid runs interspersed with buzzy notes. Robert Ridgway, in his 1889 book *Birds of Illinois*, wrote, "It is one continuous gush of sprightly music; now gay, now melodious, and then tender beyond description—the very expression of emotion."

The male defends his territory by engaging in fierce chases with intruding males. He displays for a possible mate by parading on the ground with his bill pointed up, tail spread, and wings trailing while singing fragments of his song. He places twigs at potential nest sites, but his mate constructs the actual nest of grass, twigs, and weeds, which she lines with rootlets. The site is generally in a shrub or on bare ground, often, according to Thomas S. Roberts, "beneath a canopy of silky, waving pasqueflower plumes." Preferred habitats include overgrazed pastures, sand barrens, brushy grasslands, oak savannah, and pinyon-juniper woods. The female incubates her four or five eggs for about twelve days. Both parents feed the nestlings insects and seeds that they find while walking on the ground, frequently in the company of other lark sparrows. About ten days after hatching, young birds leave the nest for the protection of shrubs.

In colonial times the lark sparrow was strictly a western bird, but in the nineteenth century it expanded eastward with the clearing of forests. Then in the twentieth century, due to urbanization, loss of grassland habitat, and reversion of agricultural areas to woods, the species again declined in the East. Roberts reported that by the early 1900s this sparrow, which once nested in all the open woodlands and prairies in Minnesota, had declined dramatically. Presently the species is widespread in the western states and much of the Midwest. In Minnesota and Wisconsin, however, it occurs only in localized areas.

On June 18, 1905, Johan Hvoslef walked from his daughter's grave in the Lanesboro cemetery across what he called the naked hill, now a golf course, where a profusion of prairie flowers grew. He wrote, "At the naked hill *Chondestes* flew off the nest when I passed. Five eggs of which one was of *Molothrus* [brown-headed cowbird]. Several *Chondestes* at full song."

In early May I usually visit Weaver Dunes, a sandy grassland preserved by the Nature Conservancy and the Minnesota Department of Natural Resources along the Mississippi River north of Winona, where lark sparrows return every year from the southwestern states or Mexico. I have looked for these birds in Fillmore County but have never found any. Although they no longer nest on Hvoslef's naked hill, I hope to find them someday on the Sand Barrens Scientific and Natural Area near Rushford.

Henslow's Sparrow

Ammodramus henslowii

The year 2005 was good for Henslow's sparrows in the Upper Midwest. Because the Hvoslef Wildlife Management Area near my home has appropriate habitat for this bird, I asked John Hockema, who is able to identify the slightest avian sound, to accompany me there. As we walked through the native grasses and nonnative brome, planted as a cover crop, John pointed a finger and said, "I hear one over there and now two more." I couldn't hear the insectlike *tsi-lick* of the elusive Henslow's until I saw one singing on top of a weed stalk. Once I connected the bird to the song, I could differentiate it from other sounds, like those of sedge wrens, and hear it, louder than expected, without John's help. Unlike the lark sparrow, the Henslow's is difficult to identify not only because of its inconspicuous vocalizations but because it is very small, usually hidden in dense grasses, and closely resembles the six other species in its genus.

Breeding takes place in wet meadows and hay fields, grassy swamps, and prairies dotted with small shrubs from western New York and Pennsylvania west to southern Minnesota, Iowa, Kansas, and Missouri. The sparrows prefer areas with standing dead vegetation and matted dead grass on the ground and avoid mowed fields or those with a lot of woody vegetation. Controlled burning that reduces woody vegetation ultimately enhances habitat but makes fields unsuitable for about two years following a burn.

A territorial male sings persistently, even through the night, from the ground or a low perch. He leads his mate to potential nest sites while carrying nesting material in his bill. The female builds a neatly woven cup of grass, often with grass arching over it, on or near the ground and incubates her three to five eggs for about eleven days. Both sexes feed their babies insects and seeds. Young birds leave the nest about ten days after hatching. In September they will join other Henslow's in migration to the southeastern states.

This sparrow, which has declined by eighty percent since 1966, is on the endangered or threatened species lists in Minnesota, Iowa, and Wisconsin and on the Audubon WatchList of highest conservation concern. Not only has it lost its original tallgrass prairie habitat but reforestation and human development have destroyed much of the remaining grasslands. However, significant populations remain in prairie remnants in Kansas, Oklahoma, and Missouri.

Ray Faber, professor of biology at Saint Mary's University in Winona, speculated that the 2005 proliferation of Henslow's reports in the Upper Midwest was due in part to an increase in the number of observers and a temporary shift north because of dry conditions elsewhere. An optimistic possibility, which seems likely because of another good year in 2006, is that expanding preservation of grasslands is helping the bird.

Harris's Sparrow

Zonotrichia querula

Occasionally during its migration, I have the pleasure of seeing an uncommon visitor in my yard; a large, distinctive sparrow with a black throat and a pinkish bill, usually in the company of its relatives the white-throated sparrows, among which another relative, the white-crowned sparrow, may be present. Sometimes I can pick out the Harris's song, which is a little like a short version of the white-throat's *old Sam Peabody, Peabody, Peabody*.

In spring the Harris's is on its way to north central Canada to nest on the edge of the tundra where the vegetation consists of stunted spruce, larch, and birch trees and shrubby willow thickets. Because of its remote breeding grounds and reclusiveness during the breeding season, the first nest of this sparrow was not discovered until 1931, long after those of most other North American birds. Nesting occurs from mid June through early July, and both sexes often return to the same territory each year. To defend his territory, the male sings persistently, usually from the top of a rock, and engages in chases with intruding males. After a quick pairing, the female, apparently alone, constructs a bulky cup nest of dead grass, moss, and lichen, which she lines with finer grass, sedges, and sometimes caribou hair. The nest is typically on the ground in a mossy depression concealed under a small tree or shrub. Following twelve to fifteen days of incubation by the female, both parents feed their nestlings, which leave the nest at eight to ten days of age.

Harris's sparrows forage for seeds, insects, and berries mostly by hopping on the ground and, like many species of sparrows, by scratching in leaf litter with their feet. In late spring berries provide most of their food. In summer they consume more insects, which they feed to their young. On wintering grounds in thickets and brushy fields and on forest edges on the Great Plains from South Dakota, southwestern Minnesota, and western Iowa to the Gulf of Mexico, seeds become central to their diet.

The isolation of this species' breeding range makes it unlikely that humans will disturb it. Winter also poses little threat to the Harris's because of its ability to use a variety of habitats and find food at an increasing number of backyard feeding stations. Nevertheless, the bird is not as common as it once was. According to Thomas S. Roberts, in the early twentieth century great numbers were present throughout Minnesota during migration, especially in the fall when the sparrows came through with their summer progeny. They were most numerous on the western prairie regions but also did "not hesitate to pass through the heavy timber of the state." Now I consider myself fortunate to see one or two every few years in my yard or in the brushy fields and woodland edges of Cardinal Marsh.

Snow Bunting

Plectrophenax nivalis

The fields with their camouflaging furrows looked empty of any living thing in November 2005 as I drove County Road 12 on my way to town. Suddenly the sky darkened with swirling flocks of birds, seeming to fly as a single entity. One flock fluttered down to the edge of the road, giving me the chance to study the birds with my binoculars. They were mostly Lapland longspurs, a sparrow that nests in the Arctic tundra and winters by the thousands mostly on windswept fields of the Great Plains. Among the thousand or more longspurs were about fifty birds that appeared mostly white with varying shades of rust on their backs and heads. I immediately recognized them as snow buntings, sparrows that also nest in the tundra.

The male of this hardy species arrives on breeding grounds and establishes a territory in early April, when temperatures still drop to twenty-two degrees below zero and snow covers most of the ground. The female arrives four to six weeks later. By this time, the male is white with a black back and the female is white with a black and gray striped back. In territorial and courtship displays the male flies up then glides down while singing. On the ground he spreads his tail and wings with his back to his mate, then makes short runs away from her. In a deep cavity or crack in a rock, the female builds a bulky cup nest of grass and moss with a thick lining of plant down, fur, and feathers to keep the eggs and babies warm. While she sits on the four to seven eggs, her mate feeds her seeds and insects that he finds while walking or running on the ground. Both parents feed their nestlings mostly insects. Young birds leave the nest when they are about two weeks old and soon form into flocks.

Snow buntings, also called snowflakes, winter on prairies, farm fields, beaches, and lake shores across most of Canada and in the United States as far south as Kansas and Missouri. They may be common in my area one winter and nonexistent another, especially if heavy snowfall buries the seeds on the tops of weeds, grasses, and sedges that are their primary sources of winter food and sends the birds farther south. The buntings and longspurs that I saw in November 2005 remained in the same area all that winter, giving me good opportunities to observe their behavior and hear the gentle, jingling warbles that are similar in both species.

Fortunately, the remote breeding range of snow buntings protects them from the effects of human activity. However, the thousands upon thousands that were present in Thomas S. Roberts's time have dwindled to flocks of lesser numbers, probably reflecting the general decrease in songbirds worldwide.

Dickcissel

Spiza americana

Soon after I began birding in 1984, I started looking for dickcissels. Several years later I was still looking for them. I knew they originally nested in prairies, so finally I visited Hayden Prairie, a two hundred forty–acre prairie remnant in northeast Iowa. There I not only found my first dickcissel but heard the bubbling songs of meadowlarks, the chattering of sedge wrens, and the shrieks of northern harriers. The diversity of plant life there equaled what Johan Hvoslef found on the prairies around Lanesboro, which have since given way to corn and soybeans.

The sparrowlike dickcissel, distinguished in the male by a yellow breast and a black V on its throat and upper chest, is a member of the family Cardinalidae and is a close relative of the indigo bunting. It is primarily a bird of the Midwest, nesting on prairies, grasslands, and cultivated and abandoned fields. Breeding locations are exceptionally erratic. Apparently in response to rainfall and its effects on habitat, the birds may occur in great numbers in a particular location one year and be absent the next.

The male arrives on his breeding grounds about a week before the female and sings to defend his territory. His only contributions to the breeding process are his genes and protection, leaving him free to have more than one mate. The female lays four eggs in dense vegetation on or near the ground in a loose cup that she has woven out of grass, leaves, and rootlets. She incubates the eggs for about thirteen days and feeds her babies mostly seeds but also some insects. During this period her own diet consists of more insects than seeds. Young birds leave the nest seven to ten days after hatching and are able to fly a few days later.

Dickcissels, which are in decline and on the Audubon WatchList, are frequent cowbird hosts, but a greater problem is the destruction of nests and nestlings by mowing machines that also threaten nests of Henslow's sparrows, bobolinks, and meadowlarks. Fortunately, some concerned farmers are timing their mowing to avoid disturbing these birds.

In Venezuela wintering dickcissels feeding on rice and sorghum may number in the millions, making them an agricultural pest and exposing them to eradication efforts. Poisoning of such large flocks could significantly reduce the world population of this bird. In response, some conservation groups have established agreements with Venezuelan farmers' associations to develop management plans for the species.

In the summers of 2005 and 2006, I saw more dickcissels in my area than ever before. They seemed to be on every fence post, power line, and weed stalk singing *dick dick ciss ciss ciss*. I watched with dread the early mowing of hay fields and gave thanks for the Hvoslef Wildlife Management Area where the birds were safe from this activity.

Western meadowlark

Eastern and Western Meadowlarks

Sturnella magna and *Sturnella neglecta*

Whenever Dana Gardner visits his hometown of Lanesboro, he comments on the scarcity of meadowlarks. "They used to be everywhere in open country," he says. Most adults, even those with little interest in birds, are able to connect spring with the songs of meadowlarks. The eastern bird sings variations of *see-you, see-you* in simple, clear, slurred whistles. The western has a longer, more melodious song that ends with a rapid gurgle. These two species are not actually larks but members of the Icteridae family, which also includes blackbirds and orioles. Their names come from their larklike preference for open country and habit of singing exuberantly on the wing.

The eastern and the western are closely related and nearly identical in appearance; the latter is slightly lighter and has more yellow on its cheek. However, in the Midwest and Southwest where their ranges overlap, the birds do not normally interbreed. Both nest in natural grasslands, abandoned weedy fields, and fields of grasslike crops such as alfalfa. The western prefers shorter grass and drier fields than the eastern. Both species forage for insects and seeds while walking on the ground and probing the soil with their bills.

To defend their territories, males sing from exposed perches. In display they point their bills up, fluff their feathers, spread their tails, and flutter straight up with legs down and wings held high. They may have more than one mate. Females build domed grass-stem nests with side entrances in depressions on the ground, interwoven with surrounding dense growth. Mothers incubate their three to seven eggs for about two weeks. When they are about twelve days old, before they are able to fly, young birds leave the nest, after which their parents continue to feed them for about two weeks. During this time the females usually begin second broods. In late fall northern birds move south. Others are permanent residents on their breeding ranges.

Over the last two decades the western meadowlark has declined dramatically on the eastern area of its range. The eastern is more common in the Upper Midwest but overall has probably declined more than its relative. Habitat destruction is to blame. In his 1999 book *Living on the Wind*, Scott Weidensaul wrote, "Taken as a whole, grassland birds have declined faster, for a longer period, and over a wider area than any other group of species." Minnesota birder Bob Janssen attributes the decline to urbanization and the proliferation of row crops. In addition, mowing of suitable habitat often occurs at the height of the breeding season. When Janssen sees thousands of hay bales in Minnesota fields, he wonders "how many nests, eggs, and young birds are wrapped in these bales." Fortunately, public lands still provide safe nesting sites.

Pine Grosbeak

Pinicola enucleator

During the winter of 1989–90 snow cover was sparse, so it was easy to walk our woodland trails. On January 2, I heard whistling calls and, in a grove of red cedar trees, spotted a flock of plump, cardinal-size birds with short dark bills. A few were pinkish red with black wings and white wingbars. Most had gray plumage with yellowish green heads and napes. I soon identified the birds as male and female pine grosbeaks. I knew this sighting was unusual, since pine grosbeaks come this far south only sporadically, so I notified Anne Marie Plunkett, who arrived the next day with Ray Glassel and Bob Janssen, both of whom, at three hundred ninety-seven species each, still tie the second-place record for the most species seen in Minnesota. The three friends found the grosbeaks in the same cedar trees where I had seen them.

North American Fringillidae, also known as winter finches, include purple finches, goldfinches, redpolls, pine grosbeaks, red crossbills, white-winged crossbills, and evening grosbeaks, among others. They are small to medium-size arboreal, seed-eating songbirds that fly fast, undulate in flight, have high-pitched calls, and gather in flocks when not nesting. As with the northern owls, patterns of movement and numbers vary greatly from year to year in response to fluctuations in food supplies, especially in winter. The birds I saw had moved south because of a poor crop of mountain ash berries, conifer seeds, and seeds of other trees across much of Canada.

Breeding locations also depend on food supplies and vary from year to year, but nesting primarily occurs in the open spruce and fir forests of Canada. The male grosbeak sings soft, whistled notes to defend his territory and in courtship feeds his mate. He remains nearby while she gathers moss, twigs, grass, lichen, and rootlets to build a bulky nest fifteen to twenty feet high on a horizontal branch or in a fork of a conifer. She sits on her two to five eggs for about two weeks. Her mate feeds her on the nest. Both parents develop throat pouches in which they carry seeds, buds, berries, and some insects to their nestlings. Young birds fledge two to three weeks after hatching.

Because of their flocking nature, these birds may be vulnerable to the spread of disease. Habitat destruction from logging operations is another concern, as are poor food crops and competition with other species.

I will always connect the 1990 occurrence of pine grosbeaks in my woods to the three expert birders who came to see them, especially Ray Glassel, a beloved Minnesota birder who has since passed away. The birds remained among the cedar trees for six weeks, allowing me and a few other visitors excellent opportunities to observe them, which was fortunate because they have not appeared in my woods again.

Red Crossbill

Loxia curvirostra

Few people would speak of a red crossbill and a northern hawk owl in the same sentence, but I will always link these birds because my only sighting of each species was on the same day: February 22, 2005. On that day, with Fred Lesher, Carol Schumacher, and Rochester birder Bill Bruins, I visited the small town of Manly in north central Iowa to see the hawk owl that had wandered far south of its normal range to spend the winter there. From Manly, we traveled west to Thorpe Park in Winnebago County, where a pair of red crossbills was in residence. As soon as we entered the park office, we saw a red, dark-winged male at a sunflower seed feeder. Soon the female arrived. She was grayish olive and yellow with dark wings.

Sunflower seeds were easy pickings for these birds compared to the work necessary for them to obtain their preferred food of seeds from evergreen cones. To reach this food they pry open the cones and spread them apart with the crossed tips of their mandibles, then lift the seeds out with their tongues. At least nine forms of red crossbills, which differ in bill size, body size, and vocalization, occur in North America. Although documentation exists for some mixed pairs, the forms do not freely interbreed, leading some researchers to suggest that all are different species. The larger-billed forms forage on larger and harder cones such as pines, while those with smaller bills forage on smaller and softer cones such as spruces, firs, and hemlocks. Buds, berries, and insects also provide food.

Crossbills are the most nomadic of all the winter finches. Time and place of nesting, generally in Canada but also in some of our northern and western states, depend on where and when cone crops are best. Breeding may occur in spring, summer, or winter. In courtship, the male sings, vibrates his wings, circles above the female, and feeds her. Far from the trunk on a horizontal branch of a conifer, the female constructs a loose cup nest of twigs, grass, moss, bark strips, feathers, and lichen. She lays three or four eggs and incubates them for about two weeks, after which she spends much time brooding the babies while the male brings food. Later, both adults feed their offspring. Young birds remain in the nest up to three weeks, during which time their mandibles gradually begin to cross.

The wandering of crossbills is most evident in winter. Range maps in field guides indicate regular occurrence throughout the country, but the greatest numbers remain in northern regions. Over the years, some forms of crossbills have decreased and others have increased, depending on the failure of certain species of cones, the logging of certain evergreens, and the introduction of competitors such as the red squirrel.

Evening Grosbeak

Coccothraustes vespertinus

One day in late fall 1984 I saw a bird at my feeder that I had never seen before. It had a huge bill and a plump body and looked to me like a giant goldfinch. I thought it was an anomaly, maybe a goldfinch with an abnormal amount of growth hormone. When my excitement subsided, I carefully studied a field guide and identified the bird as an evening grosbeak. Soon about thirty of these birds arrived and stayed until February 19, 1985. They were voracious, noisy eaters, sounding somewhat like house sparrows, and intermingled constantly with little apparent fear of humans. On October 9, 1985, they returned and ate their way through vast amounts of sunflower seeds until April 25, 1986.

Evening grosbeaks generally forage in trees and shrubs for a variety of seeds, berries, and insects. They have a close predator-prey relationship with a pulpwood forest pest, the spruce budworm, feeding heavily on budworm larvae, which they also feed to their young. Breeding takes place in spruce, fir, pine, and mixed forests of southern Canada, a few northern states, and the mountainous regions of some western states. A courting male with head and tail raised crouches low, fluffs his feathers, quivers his wings, and swivels back and forth. He frequently feeds his mate and engages in alternate bowing with her. On a horizontal branch or vertical fork of a tree, the female builds a loose cup nest of twigs, which she lines with fine grass, pine needles, rootlets, and moss. During the eleven to fourteen days that she incubates three or four eggs, her mate may feed her on the nest. Both adults feed the nestlings. Fledging occurs about two weeks after hatching.

In response to the availability of food, evening grosbeaks wander widely and erratically in winter and have occurred throughout the country at one time or another. Beginning in the late nineteenth century, they steadily wandered east from their original home in the foothills of the Canadian Rocky Mountains, where they received their name from English settlers who mistakenly believed the birds came out of the woods to sing only after sundown. During the winter of 1889–90 great flocks reached New England but then didn't return for twenty more years. Populations were slightly increasing until the last major outbreak of spruce budworms ended in the 1970s, after which numbers began to decline, especially in the Northeast and Great Lakes regions.

The last time I saw these gregarious birds with big bills and big appetites was November 10, 1987, when two individuals appeared and stayed for only one day. I still watch for them every year but with little hope. One theory for their absence in my area is that the birds, which still occur in moderate numbers, are finding sufficient food at sunflower seed feeders farther north.

RECOMMENDED READING

The following online resources offer current information about organizations that focus directly on birds or indirectly affect birds through conservation. Home pages usually provide general information with links to member services and publications. In addition, they may direct viewers to initiatives, programs, and other sections, many of which encourage online participation. These addresses may change over time. New addresses are easy to find by entering the name of the organization through a search engine.

I have also selected a variety of books and journals that will be of interest to beginning, casual, or avid birdwatchers, focusing on such topics as identification, the lives of birds, migration, conservation, avian biology, and scientific studies.

ONLINE RESOURCES
National and International Organizations

AMERICAN BIRD CONSERVANCY
http://www.abcbirds.org

The ABC's mission is to conserve wild birds and their habitats throughout the Americas. Working extensively with other organizations, the ABC is dedicated solely to identifying and overcoming the greatest threats facing birds in the Western Hemisphere.

The home page has links to programs, alliances, and campaigns such as the Bird Conservation Alliance, a forum for organizations to exchange ideas regarding conservation issues; Climate Change, which describes the already apparent and potential effects of global warming on birds; International, a program that builds networks between North America, Latin America, and the Caribbean for bird conservation; Pesticides, which explains the effects of pesticides on birds and strategies to reduce exposure; and Partners in Flight, a cooperative effort by conservation organizations dedicated to the long-term health of land birds that breed in the United States.

AMERICAN BIRDING ASSOCIATION
http://www.americanbirding.org

The ABA specifically caters to recreational birders by increasing their knowledge, skills, and enjoyment of birding. It provides information on identification and listing, promotes responsible birding through a code of ethics, and encourages the conservation of birds and their habitats.

The home page has a search engine and good links to Events, including ABA-endorsed tours; Young Birders, including information on conferences, camps, and scholarships; Resources, including the ABA checklist, clubs, festivals, and trails; and ABA Sales.

AMERICAN ORNITHOLOGISTS' UNION
http://www.aou.org

Founded in 1883, the AOU is the oldest organization in the New World devoted to the scientific study of birds. Although primarily for professional ornithologists, it welcomes as members anyone interested in birds.

Some good home page links are to checklists, including one for North American birds that is the accepted authority for English bird names and scientific nomenclature; Resources, which includes a variety of scientific literature; Awards; and Committees.

BIRDLIFE INTERNATIONAL
http://www.birdlife.org

Based in the United Kingdom, BirdLife International is a global partnership of conservation organizations that promotes sustainability in the use of natural resources and works to conserve birds, their habitats, and global biodiversity. It publishes a valuable yearly report on the state of the world's birds and is the founder and coordinator of the Important Bird Areas program, which identifies critical habitats.

Two of the most helpful home page links are Action and Data Zone. Action directs the viewer to such sections as Action Index, Campaigns, Conservation Science, and Building Awareness. Data Zone offers fact sheets on every species worldwide, information about significant sites, and case studies.

CORNELL LAB OF ORNITHOLOGY
http://www.birds.cornell.edu

The Lab's mission is to interpret and conserve the earth's biological diversity through research, education, and citizen science focused on birds. Programs work with government agencies, nongovernmental agencies, and individuals of all ages and skill levels across North America and beyond.

The most useful link on Cornell's home page is Lab Programs, from which you can access Citizen Science, listing all the programs that involve individual participation. For example, eBird, a valuable tool for birdwatchers and conservationists, allows individuals not only to enter into a database all the birds they see in North America but to access the entire database to learn what others are reporting. Some of the other citizen science projects are Birds in Forested Landscapes, the Great Backyard Bird Count, and Project FeederWatch.

DUCKS UNLIMITED
http://www.ducks.org

Although DU's emphasis is on ducks and hunting, its initiatives to conserve, restore, and manage wetlands and associated habitats for North America's waterfowl also benefit other wildlife and people. Since the 1930s, the organization has restored and conserved almost twelve million acres of crucial habitat.

The home page directs the viewer to the Wetlands for Tomorrow campaign, a continental effort to raise $1.7 billion for wetland conservation in North America's grasslands, forests, coastal marshes, and strategic locations such as the Mississippi River floodplain.

INTERNATIONAL CRANE FOUNDATION
http://www.savingcranes.org

The ICF works worldwide to conserve cranes and the wetland and grassland ecosystems on which they depend. It focuses on endangered-species management, wetland ecology, habitat restoration, and the critical need for international cooperation. The foundation maintains a collection of captive cranes for the purposes of breeding and reintroduction into the wild.

The home page has buttons to the following sites: Educators and Kids, Conservation and Research, Photo Gallery, Whooping Crane Reintroduction Updates, and Species Field Guide, which contains natural histories of fifteen crane species.

NATIONAL AUDUBON SOCIETY
http://www.audubon.org

Audubon has a national network of community-based nature centers, chapters, and scientific and educational programs. Its mission is to conserve and restore natural ecosystems, with a focus on birds.

The home page has a link to Birds and Science, with directions to Bird Conservation and from there to two important sites, the Audubon WatchList, which identifies and gives natural histories of species that need help, and Important Bird Areas, a program that works with BirdLife International to identify critical habitats. The Birds and Science button also directs the viewer to Citizen Science and from there to the Great Backyard Bird Count, in cooperation with Cornell, and the Christmas Bird Count, in which more than fifty thousand observers participate each year.

NATIONAL WILDLIFE FEDERATION
http://www.nwf.org

The NWF is the largest American conservation organization. Its mission is to "inspire Americans to protect wildlife for our children's future." Main areas of focus are connecting people to nature, reversing global warming (in partnership with the American Bird Conservancy), and protecting and restoring critical wildlife habitats.

Some home page links are Global Warming; Outside in Nature; Wildlife, which gives the status and brief natural histories of some endangered animals; and eNature.com, a site that offers natural histories of many species for a fee.

NATURE CONSERVANCY
http://www.nature.org

This organization works with partners, corporations, indigenous peoples, and traditional communities to protect the most ecologically important lands and waters worldwide. Its mission is to preserve the natural communities that represent the diversity of life on earth.

The home page directs the viewer to News Room, Where We Work, and How We Work. I found How We Work the most interesting. It includes Nature Travel options; Private Lands Conservation; Conservation Methods; and initiatives such as Fire, Climate Change, Freshwater, Marine, and Invasive Species.

SIERRA CLUB
http://www.sierraclub.org

The Sierra Club is a grassroots organization working to protect communities and the planet. Its mission is to "explore, enjoy, and protect the wild places of the earth; practice and promote the responsible use of the earth's ecosystems and resources; educate and enlist humanity to protect and restore the quality of the natural and human environment; and use all lawful means to carry out these objectives."

Among other sites, the home page directs the viewer to Our Conservation Initiatives, under which are Smart Energy Solutions, Safe and Healthy Communities, America's Wild Legacy, and More Programs. Each section has links to more detailed information.

State Departments of Natural Resources

Department of Natural Resources sites for each state provide information on parks, wildlife areas, endangered and threatened species, regulations for hunting and fishing, management plans, research, and other topics. Links to various departments, such as ecological services or nongame programs, are especially helpful.

Illinois Department of Natural Resources
http://www.dnr.state.il.us

Indiana Department of Natural Resources
http://www.in.gov/dnr

Iowa Department of Natural Resources
http://www.iowadnr.com

Michigan Department of Natural Resources
http://www.michigan.gov/dnr

Minnesota Department of Natural Resources
http://www.dnr.state.mn.us/index.html

North Dakota Game and Fish Department
http://www.gf.nd.gov

Ohio Department of Natural Resources
http://www.dnr.state.oh.us

South Dakota Game, Fish and Parks
http://www.sdgfp.info

Wisconsin Department of Natural Resources
http://www.dnr.wi.gov

State Birding Organizations
and Electronic Mailing Lists

Web sites for these organizations contain information relevant to the birds in each specific state, including Upper Midwest birding hotspots, birding events, books about the state's birds, checklists of species that occur in the state, lists of species at risk, and distribution maps for migratory, breeding, and year-round residents. They may also allow for individual electronic seasonal reports.

Subscribers to electronic mailing lists (e-mail lists) post sightings, ask questions, and generate discussions. They in turn receive daily e-mails from people who wish to do the same. E-mail lists are the quickest way to spread the word about the presence of certain birds. They are also the primary sources of rare bird alerts. Archives allow viewing of all postings.

Illinois Ornithological Society
Web site: http://www.illinoisbirds.org
IL Birders' Exchanging Thoughts E-mail list:
    http://www.groups.yahoo.com/group/Ilbirds

Indiana Audubon Society
Web site: http://www.indianaaudubon.org

Iowa Ornithologists' Union
Web site: http://www.iowabirds.org
E-mail list: http://www.iowabirds.org/IOU/IA-BIRD.asp

Michigan Birds Network
Web site: http://www.michiganbirds.org

Minnesota Ornithologists' Union
Web site: http://www.moumn.org
E-mail list: http://www.moumn.org/listservice.html

MnBird
Web site and e-mail list: http://www.mnbird.net
Encourages reports of all sightings and is especially welcoming to novice birders.

North Dakota Birding Society
Web site: http://www.ndbirdingsociety.com
E-mail list: http://listserve.nodak.edu/archives/nd-birds.html

Ohio Ornithological Society
Web site: http://www.ohiobirds.org/index.php
E-mail list: http://www.lists.envirolink.ore/mailman/listsinfo/ohio-birds

South Dakota Ornithologists' Union
Web site: http://www.homepages.dsu.edu/palmerj/SDOU/about.html
E-mail list: subscribe to majordomo@igc.org

Wisconsin Society for Ornithology
Web site: http://www.uwgb.edu/birds/wso
E-mail list: subscribe to j.thomas.sykes@lawrence.edu

PUBLICATIONS
Books

Beadle, David, and James D. Rising. *Sparrows of the United States and Canada: The Photographic Guide*. San Diego: Academic Press, 1996. The first part of the book consists of concise yet detailed species accounts that cover identification, voice, history, geographic variations, measurements, and other attributes. The second part contains color illustrations of up to as many as eight different plumages per species.

Bent, Arthur Cleveland. Life Histories of North American Birds series. 21 vols. Washington, D.C.: United States Government Printing Office, 1919–1968. This series by Bent and his collaborators consists of comprehensive species accounts that provided a foundation for all the compilations of North American bird biology that followed. An electronic collection of selected species is available at http://www.birdsbybent.com.

Curson, Jon, David Quinn, and David Beadle. *Warblers of the Americas: An Identification Guide*. Boston: Houghton Mifflin, 1994. Color plates in the first half of the book show plumage variations in exceptionally good detail. Range maps are mediocre. Text in the second half of the book gives detailed descriptions of all plumages with lesser information on other attributes.

Dunne, Pete, David Sibley, and Clay Sutton. *Hawks in Flight: The Flight Identification of North American Migrant Raptors*. Boston: Houghton Mifflin, 1988. Drawings of North American raptors in flight show variations in plumage and excellent comparisons between species. The text offers good introductions to each group of raptors and for each species provides descriptions of its appearance and behavior, along with comparisons to similar species.

Ehrlich, Paul R., David S. Dobkin, and Darryl Wheye. *The Birder's Handbook*. New York: Simon and Schuster, 1988. On even-numbered pages, this guide to the natural history of North American birds gives brief narratives of each species' breeding biology, diet, and conservation. Essays on odd-numbered pages cover a range of topics, a few of which are bird names, the avian sense of smell, walking versus hopping, and bills.

Erickson, Laura. *101 Ways to Help Birds*. Mechanicsburg, Pennsylvania: Stackpole Books, 2006. Erickson's important, timely, and well-written book details all the threats that avian life is facing and offers practical ways to help birds and ourselves as well. What I like best are her clear, understandable explanations of complex issues such as pollution, land management, insecticides, and global warming.

Farrand, John, Jr. ed. *The Audubon Society Master Guide to Birding*. 3 vols. New York: Knopf, 1983. Short introductions to each family of birds are helpful. Species accounts include identifying characteristics and comparisons with similar species. One or more photographs are on facing pages.

Gill, Frank B. *Ornithology*. New York: W. H. Freeman, 1995. *Ornithology* is the best available textbook on the scientific study and biology of birds. Although written for undergraduate students, it is a valuable resource for anyone wanting in-depth knowledge of the origins of birds, their form and function, behavior and communication, and reproduction and development.

Karalus, Karl E., and Allan W. Eckert. *The Owls of North America (North of Mexico)*. Garden City, New York: Doubleday, 1974. The authors present detailed descriptions and natural histories of all North American owls, treating such topics as eyes and vision, ears and hearing, voice, longevity, shape at rest and in flight, weight and measurements, and carrying of prey. Drawings and full-page color portraits accompany the text.

Kaufman, Kenn. *Lives of North American Birds*. Boston: Houghton Mifflin, 1996. This book is one of my favorites. It contains summaries of feeding, nesting, and displays for each family of birds. The individual species accounts are succinct yet thorough, covering preferred habitats, diet, foraging methods, defense of territory, courtship rituals, nests, eggs, young birds, migration, range, and conservation status.

Leahy, Christopher W. *The Birdwatcher's Companion: An Encyclopedic Handbook of North American Birdlife*. New York: Hill and Wang, 1982. Organized alphabetically, this book presents essays on an array of subjects, some of which are aggression, bathing, duetting, drunkenness, evolution, feathers, intelligence, navigation, nomadism, nomenclature, parental care, play, and sleep.

Pearson, T. Gilbert, et al., eds. *Birds of America*. Garden City, New York: Doubleday, 1917. The color plates skillfully depict several species together in their preferred habitats. Introductions to orders and families are thorough. Interesting alternate common names are given for each species as well as brief descriptions of appearance, nest and eggs, and distribution, followed by delightful anecdotes from contributing authors.

Poole, Alan, and Frank B. Gill, eds. *The Birds of North America*. 18 vols. New York: Cambridge University Press, 2002. This joint project of the American Ornithologists' Union, the Cornell Lab of Ornithology, and the Academy of Natural Sciences is the most current and comprehensive source for the natural histories of species nesting in the United States and Canada. It is also available by subscription online at http://www.bna.birds.cornell.edu/BNA.

Roberts, Thomas S. *The Birds of Minnesota*. 2 vols. Minneapolis: University of Minnesota Press, 1932. Minnesota birders frequently refer to this well-illustrated book for the historical occurrence and abundance of birds in the state. Following basic descriptions are personal anecdotes and reports by the author and from other birders such as Johan C. Hvoslef, the Lanesboro, Minnesota, physician and naturalist who recorded all the birds he saw in Fillmore County from 1881 to 1918.

Sherman, Althea R. *Birds of an Iowa Dooryard*. Iowa City: University of Iowa Press, 1996. Originally published in 1952 by Arthur J. Palas, *Birds of an Iowa Dooryard* is a lively narrative by one of Iowa's most interesting bird enthusiasts. Sherman offers an intimacy with the avian world and an understanding of ecological processes as she describes her studies of the chimney swifts and other birds that inhabited her one-acre property in northeastern Iowa.

Sibley, David Allen. *The Sibley Guide to Bird Life and Behavior*. New York: Knopf, 2001. Rather than describing the natural history of each species as Kaufman does, Sibley provides information that is more general. In part one he discusses characteristics that apply to all birds. In part two he discusses birds as families, including such topics as taxonomy, food and foraging, courtship displays, nests, eggs, young birds, migration patterns, and conservation.

Sibley, David Allen. *The Sibley Guide to Birds*. New York: Knopf, 2000. Although too large to carry into the field, this book is the definitive identification guide for experienced birders. Illustrations highlight unique markings and show plumage variations and birds in flight. Group accounts show all species in a family on one or two pages. Range maps are excellent.

Skutch, Alexander F. *Life of the Tanager*. Ithaca: Cornell University Press, 1989. Only four species of tanagers regularly breed in North America, but about two hundred brightly colored species varying from red to blue, green, and purple occur in Central and South America. In this book, exquisitely illustrated by Dana Gardner, Skutch tells the stories of these birds.

Skutch, Alexander F. *Parent Birds and Their Young*. Austin: University of Texas Press, 1976. In his most comprehensive book, Skutch relates thoroughly researched accounts of parenting by birds worldwide. He includes personal experiences and theories along with reports and anecdotes from other ornithologists.

Stokes, Donald W., and Lillian Q. Stokes. *A Guide to Bird Behavior*. 3 vols. Boston: Little, Brown, 1979. The Stokes guides are the best references I have found for interpreting visual and vocal displays of certain common species. They also include information on the establishment of territories, courtship, nest building, incubation, care of young birds, and seasonal movement.

Weidensaul, Scott. *Living on the Wind: Across the Hemisphere with Migratory Birds*. New York: North Point Press, 1999. The author describes difficult scientific concepts in a way that makes them accessible to the lay person, interweaving them with personal experiences that make the book read like an adventure. With conservation as his strongest theme, Weidensaul discusses all the perils that migratory birds face, along with efforts to help them.

State Atlases of Breeding Bird Surveys

These books present detailed records, including range maps, of the composition and distribution of species breeding in the particular states. They provide baseline data for environmental monitoring and future comparisons of changes in bird life. Atlases are not available for Minnesota or North Dakota.

Brewer, Richard, Gail A. McPeek, and Raymond J. Adams, Jr. *The Atlas of Breeding Birds of Michigan*. East Lansing: Michigan State University Press, 1991. A second survey will be completed in 2007.

Castrale, John S., Edward M. Hopkins, and Charles E. Keller. *The Indiana Breeding Bird Atlas*. Indianapolis: Indiana Department of Natural Resources, 1998. A second survey will be completed in 2010.

Cutright, Noel J., Bette R. Harriman, and Robert W. Howe. *Atlas of the Breeding Birds of Wisconsin*. Waukesha: Wisconsin Society for Ornithology, 2006.

Jackson, Laura Spess, Carol A. Thompson, and James J. Dinsmore. *The Iowa Breeding Bird Atlas*. Iowa City: University of Iowa Press, 1996.

Kleen, Vernon M., Liane Cordle, and Robert A. Montgomery. *The Illinois Breeding Bird Atlas*. Chicago: Illinois Natural History Survey, 2004.

Peterjohn, Bruce G., and Daniel L. Rice. *The Ohio Breeding Bird Atlas*. Columbus: Ohio Department of Natural Resources, 1991. Work on a second atlas is under way.

Peterson, Richard A. *The South Dakota Breeding Bird Atlas*. Aberdeen: South Dakota Ornithologists' Union, 1995.

Journals

The national and international organizations listed in the online resources have their own publications in the forms of magazines and newsletters that present valuable information either directly or indirectly related to birds. State birding organizations issue journals consisting of seasonal reports, scientific papers, and notes of interest. They may also provide newsletters that are less formal.

Typical examples of a journal and newsletter are the *Loon* and *Minnesota Birding*, both published by the Minnesota Ornithologists' Union. These publications have given me access to some of the references used for this book, including Kim Eckert's overview of the 2004–05 influx of northern owls, Judy Englund's article about ospreys in the Twin Cities, Bruce Fall and James Mattsson's reports of interbreeding between summer tanagers and scarlet tanagers, Bob Janssen's discussion of the western meadowlark, and Pam Perry's article about loons and lead poisoning.

INDEX